African Heartbeat

Transatlantic Literary and Cultural Dynamics

Nancy Ann Watanabe

Hamilton Books

Lanham • Boulder • New York • Toronto • Plymouth, UK

Copyright © 2018 by Hamilton Books
4501 Forbes Boulevard, Suite 200, Lanham, Maryland 20706
Hamilton Books Acquisitions Department (301) 459-3366

Unit A, Whitacre Mews, 26-34 Stannary Street,
London SE11 4AB, United Kingdom

The quotation from *The No. 1 Ladies' Detective Agency* in the epigraph to chapter 1 is
reprinted by permission of Alexander McCall Smith.

Printed in the United States of America
British Library Cataloguing in Publication Information Available

Library of Congress Control Number: 2017953736
ISBN: 978-0-7618-7006-7 (cloth : alk. paper)—ISBN: 978-0-7618-7007-4 (electronic)

♾™ The paper used in this publication meets the minimum requirements of American
National Standard for Information Sciences Permanence of Paper for Printed Library
Materials, ANSI/NISO Z39.48-1992.

Contents

Chapter One

African-American Heroism in *Uncle Tom's Cabin* and *Enemy of the State*

Mma Ramotswe thought: God put us on this earth. We were all Africans then, in the beginning, because man started in Kenya, as Dr. Leakey and his Daddy have proved. So, if one thinks carefully about it, we are all brothers and sisters. . . . and it [is] wrong to lie, and steal, and kill other people.
—Alexander McCall Smith (*No. 1 Ladies' Detective Agency* 35-36)

I am the darker brother.
They send me to eat in the kitchen
When company comes,
But I laugh,
And eat well,
And grow strong.
—Langston Hughes, "I, Too, Sing America" (*CP* 46)

Persistence of vision may be theorized to be the root cause that explains why armed law enforcement officers have been involved in tragic fatalities while in pursuit of unarmed young African-American suspects. Elizabeth Ammons and Susan Belasco observe, "Perhaps one of the central and most worthwhile challenges in teaching *Uncle Tom's Cabin* lies in finding ways to discuss the book's racism not simply as a historical phenomenon, important as that is, but also as a force operating in and intersecting with issues in our own world" (2). In my view, America has been haunted in recent years by the cloying tenacity of the Plantation Era Fugitive Slave laws, which, *Uncle Tom's Cabin, or Life among the Lowly* shows and *Enemy of the State* suggests, were unethical and immoral, seething beneath a geopolitically configured slick surface of legality, but so essentially inhumane and controversial as to erupt in the armed violence of civil war. A cornerstone concept in this chapter is *persistence of vision*, which designates the way the mind retains images mirrored on the eye's retina during an ordinary act of apprehension involving basic sensory perception of seeing a person, place, thing, or action that actually exists or occurs in the confines of one's immediate environment. *Persistence of vision* explains why audiences view rapidly flowing motion picture frames, not disjointed images jumping from one to the next, but a continuous stream of images that display continuity and coherence similar to the way things happen in actual life. "To persist" denotes "to continue firmly in a state or action in spite of obstacles or objection" (*Webster's*). "Vision" refers to "the act or faculty of seeing external objects; sight; thing seen; imaginary sight; phantom; imaginative insight or foresight." The adjective "visionary" denotes "apt to see visions; indulging in fancy or reverie; impractical; existing only in the imagination." Especially among literary aficionados connoting positive traits of character, "visionary" refers to a person who is "prone to see visions." My approach to "visionary" carries both positive and negative connotations. I view *pernicious persistence of vision* as a covert perpetrator of interracial urban violence. Symptomatic of a blight on twenty-first century America, tragic incidents hit the streets and neighborhoods of America during 2012-2015, forging victims of Trayvon Martin in Miami Gardens, Florida, on February 26, 2012; Michael Brown in Ferguson, Missouri, on August 9, 2014; and Walter Scott in North Charleston, South Carolina, on April 4, 2015. National and international televised news broadcasts of sudden deaths of these young African-American men suggest iconic imagery reminiscent of the Runaway Slave archetype popularized by satirical humorist Mark Twain in *Huckleberry Finn* (1884). As a caveat to the adage that we should study tragic incidents in American history to avoid repeating them, I suggest that unguided, or worse, misguided exposure to socially constructed racial stereotypes in the historical continuum fosters injurious brainwashing, perpetuating indelible images that reside as invisible perpetrators acting undetected on persons without conscious knowledge of how such images affect their reflex actions in crisis situations requiring an instantaneous response. My analysis of Harriet Beecher Stowe's controversial antebellum novel and Tony Scott's popular contemporary film tackles this contemporary American issue—instantaneous use of fatal force against unarmed suspects, young black men not confronting patrolmen but running away from armed white men—which has reached crisis proportions. My discussion of *persistence of vision* in art and life contributes to ongoing dialoguing generated by needless tragic deaths that undermine effectiveness of law enforcement peace officers in America.

"Escape," observes Kristin Herzog, is "the means to overcome violence in *Uncle Tom's Cabin*, although Stowe's 'romantic racialism' celebrates the nonescaping Tom more than any other figure in the story" (139). But Uncle Tom is a heroic Christian martyr, and many African-Americans shun Uncle Tom, preferring escapee George Harris. David Millward reports, "America has to escape from the residual racism which has scarred its history, President Barack Obama said last night" (Web). I interpret this "residual racism" as a manifestation of *persistence of vision* that counterpoints the artistically depicted Runaway Slave archetype. Although the powerful Fugitive Slave Law of 1850 was rescinded in 1864, decisions to take corrective action were based on battlefield victories, not reasoned argument and negotiation. Legislatively abolishing slavery and outlawing racial discrimination in the Civil Rights Act of 1964 have not healed deep-seated psychological wounds, letting the image of Runaway Slave fester in the minds, and dictate the conditioned behavioral reflex actions, of both black Americans and white Americans. Historically, accounts of runaway slaves in antebellum America (1812-1861) struck people's minds, perpetuating negative *persistence of vision*, which manifests in more positive constructions when detectable as an artistically shaped motif. *Persistence of vision* wields long-drawn-out power in imaginative works by Stowe, Twain, and Scott, facilitating discussion about complicated art-life parallels that suggest the haunting of twenty-first-century America by the prevailing rule of law in antebellum America.

Both Stowe and Scott evince profound interest in racial issues at the core of the American Civil War. Harriet Beecher was a Northerner educated in the 1820s in Hartford, Connecticut. While residing in Cincinnati, Ohio, 1832-1849, she married best friend Eliza Tyler Stowe's widowed (by cholera) husband Reverend Calvin Ellis Stowe on January 6, 1836. Cincinnati was "a Southern city on Northern soil" located on the Ohio River, known as "the Jordan between slavery and freedom" (Kirkham 19). To deprecate the 1850 Fugitive Slave Law, Harriet Beecher Stowe (1811-1896) wrote *Uncle Tom's Cabin* in New Brunswick, Maine, where Reverend Stowe taught at Bowdoin College. E. Bruce Kirkham observes that Stowe wrote "with the voice of authority," using minute details to create local color, a sense of reality, and building "trust" in her portrayals in the first half of *Uncle Tom Cabin's*, while the novel's second half shifts to the Deep South and maintains "the same technique of minute detail, even though she had never been there" (68). Stowe read about and observed slavery's victims, resulting in a double-fisted yet even-handed exposé. Stowe presented "a balanced picture of slavery," both "the *best side* of the thing, and something *faintly approaching the worst*" (Kirkham 67). Stowe's pictorial editing techniques augmented straightforward storytelling, anticipating American novelists' "film aesthetic" (Magny) and American jazz's improvisatory collaboration and "integration of performance into the social fabric" (Gioia 9).

At a time when profiteering slave traders legally separated black families, executed white dissenters, and shot runaways on sight, Stowe's political novel bravely appraised slavery, open-mindedly portraying Negro slaves and Southern plantation slaveholders as pawns, victims of ruthless slave traders mandated by Southern socioeconomic infrastructure to flout plummeting moral values, allowing a white majority to reap profits on the backs of unremunerated field laborers and domestic help. Following serialization in the anti-slavery magazine *National Era* (June 5, 1851-March 13, 1852), *Uncle Tom's Cabin* was a best-seller at 300,000 copies upon publication as a book in 1852, which suggests literate America felt an unmet need to reexamine an institution that assured affluence for privileged Southern families, descendants of British colonists, e.g., Jamestown Royal Colony (1607)[1] , Mayflower Pilgrim Plymouth Colony (1620), and Rhode Island Charter Colony (1636). African slave traders encouraged transatlantic commerce in slave labor, and African auctioneers often separated families when they categorically, on demand, sold men, women, and children in transatlantic expansion of the African market, enabling Southeast Atlantic American farmers to build an agrarian empire. During the Middle Passage, 1500-1800, white planters harvested cotton, sugar, tobacco, and coffee cash crops, capitalizing on labor procured from West African Gold Coast exporters and financed by the British Empire. New England made rum using sugar imported from the Caribbean, which then traded slaves for rum (Harris xiii). Harms incurred by these thriving regional American business enterprises got swept along, often tolerated as extensions of Manifest Destiny doctrine making America *the* land of opportunity. Southern slaveholders did not dislike Negroes; indeed, Southerners depended on Negroes, many embraced as beloved family members, beyond ordinary domestic helpers' and laborers' expectations. *Uncle Tom's Cabin* shows America at a crossroads where prosperity for agrarian white Southerners is a rising profit line representing systemic economic gain in the U.S. slave economy of more than $3.5 billion (Scott and Scott, *Gettysburg*), unfavorably intersecting with moral regression into systematic exploitation and oppression of slaves whose loss of human rights to earn a decent wage and raise a family subjected them to dehumanization and rampant injustice; *Uncle Tom's Cabin*'s earliest subtitle was *The Man That Was a Thing.* Stowe moralizes but she also lets the words, thoughts and actions of emblematic characters point to gaps between legal and ethical imperatives. Her seminal portrayal of ethnic diversity and political pluralism enriched American culture, instigating Reconstruction, 1865-1895. In 1862, when President Abraham Lincoln met Mrs. Stowe, he praised her contribution in furthering the cause of civil rights. Joan Hedrick recounts that when Lincoln was introduced to Stowe, he said, "So you're the little woman who wrote the book that started this Great War!" (vii). But I regard *Uncle Tom's Cabin* as a monument promulgating the idea that discourse is the only pathway to resolution of ideological gridlock, not civil war.

MLA International Bibliography currently lists 108 articles on Tony Scott's oeuvre (e.g., Cobley on *Enemy of the State*). Critics praise British movie director Tony Scott as "an impeccable stylist" whose "kinetic style ushered in a generation of filmmakers that couldn't seem to sit still" ("Remembering"). This chapter examines the artistry of *Enemy of the State,* probing its geopolitical heart and historical soul to illuminate morally informed depth perception in Scott's "visual style," "fast cuts," and "high energy approach" ("Remembering"). A commercial film director in the 1970s, Scott arrived in Hollywood in the 1980s. Scott's *Enemy of the State* uses film art to cultivate political dynamism, quasi poetical imagery, and keen-eyed portraiture of societal milieu, comparable to Stowe's artistry in *Uncle Tom's Cabin.* Initially, *Enemy of the State* suggests a prevailing consciousness among mainstream Americans of virtually no difference between persons of black racial origins and white racial origins. Scott's portrayal of the African-American protagonist in *Enemy of the State* is deeply rooted in Stowe's depiction of Sam, who has "a comprehensiveness of vision and a strict lookout to his own personal well-being that would have done credit to any white patriot in Washington" (Stowe 59-60), suggestive of racial equality, i.e., African-American self-esteem rooted 100% in black values incorporating, not opposing, white American values. Obliquely, Scott's film compares African-American protagonist Robert Clayton Dean [Will Smith], typifying a prosperous Washington attorney and family man, to John Wesley Dean, III (b. 1938), a White House Counsel (July 1970-April 1973) who unknowingly participated in the Watergate burglaries; as the prosecution's star witness he pled guilty to masterminding a cover-up. Inadvertently, protagonist Robert Clayton Dean is short-circuited into a maelstrom of politically-motivated malfeasance perpetrated by fanatical Thomas Brian Reynolds [Jon Voight], advisor to National Security Agency (NSA) Deputy Director of Operations, whom he aims to supplant by falsifying Federal Bureau of Investigation approval and forcing Congress to endorse his electronic surveillance expansion by buying votes for a bogus Telecommunications Security and Privacy Act. As Simon Legree is a cruel enemy within slavery's stranglehold, so, too, Reynolds is a crooked politician infiltrating a military-industrial complex. While Robert Clayton Dean's blackness has no apparent connection to the political plot, screenwriter David Marconi artistically incorporates serendipitous occurrences signaling the invisible presence of the playful and unpredictable African "trickster" divinity Esu-Elegbara.[2] Conversely, Thomas Brian Reynolds symbolizes the irreverent and nihilistic Norse mythological trickster god Loki, who killed Fimafeng, a slave. Snorri Sturluson (1179-1241) explains, "Loki is pleasing, even beautiful to look at, but his nature is evil and he is undependable. More than others, he has the kind of wisdom known as cunning, and is treacherous in all matters. He constantly places the gods in difficulties and often solves their problems with guile!" (39). The epithet "trickster" carries upbeat connotations in African cosmology, but pessimistic meanings in Norse mythology.

Scott's oft-televised feature film begins shockingly with a congressional U.S. lawmaker being killed by a corrupt security advisor, then segues to an ornithologist discovering the murder filmed by his camera, saving (hot-swapping) it to a video-diskette ("NEC" Nippon Electric Corp.) seconds before being violently chased by thugs under technocrat Fiedler [Jack Black] deploying satellite-driven surveillance cameras overseeing metropolitan Washington. Scott embeds in this action-packed suspense thriller a key image to evoke the iconic archetype of Runaway Slave. In *Enemy of the State* (1998), Tony Scott, a longtime Los Angeles resident, depicts America from his semi-objective vantage point as a native of the United Kingdom. Born in North Shields, England, Tony (Anthony David Leighton) Scott (1944-2012) devoted his directorial career to portraying American culture, starting with his Hollywood-style feature film *Top Gun* (1986), followed by *Days of Thunder* (1990), *Revenge* (1990), *The Last Boy Scout* (1991), *True Romance* (1993), *Crimson Tide* (1995), *The Fan* (1996), *Man on Fire* (2004), *The Taking of Pelham 123* (2009), and *Unstoppable* (2010). His first experience in the filmmaking industry was as a teenager starring in *Boy and Bicycle*, directed by his older brother, Ridley Scott, who went on to make blockbuster movies *Alien* (1979), *Blade Runner* (1982), *Black Rain* (1989), *Thelma and Louise* (1991), and *Gladiator* (2000). In a variant of Alfred Hitchcock's jazzy[3] signature offbeat appearances syncopating films including *Spellbound* (1945), *To Catch a Thief* (1955), *Wrong Man* (1956), and *Vertigo* (1958), *Enemy of the State*'s portrayal of fleeing Jewish-American bicyclist Daniel Leon Zavitz [Jason Lee], a Messiah Christ-figure in *Enemy of the State*, suggests an autobiographical allusion to *Boy and Bicycle*, indicating Scott sympathetically constructs archetypal imagery rooted in Jewish exodus from Egypt via the Red Sea into Israel. Nigerian poet Abioseh Davidson Nicol's lyrics poignantly dovetail with birdwatcher Daniel Leon Zavitz:

> The pedaling cyclist wavers by
> On the wrong side of the road,
> As if uncertain of his new emancipation.
> I know now that is what you are, Africa:
> Happiness, contentment, and fulfillment,
> And a small bird singing in a mango tree. (9, 10)

Similarly to the way Robert Clayton Dean represents African-American descendants of Negro slaves, Daniel Leon Zavitz emblematizes Hebraic tribes of Israel, slaves who were empire builders of the imperial Egyptian pharaohs' pyramids.

The African-American spirit of free play is a key signature of democracy in the United States of America. Critical collocation of *Uncle Tom's Cabin* and *Enemy of the State* suggests dovetailing of Stowe's anticipatory advocacy of the black sentiment "I, too, am America" (*CP* 46) expressed by 1920s "towering influence" Langston Hughes (Glaser 419) and Scott's hitherto unrecognized yet rather perceptive insight into the crucial role of African culture in facilitating the democratic process in America, from the intricacies of the electoral college aligned with casting votes on Election Day to the formal ritual of the nonpartisan referee's coin toss to decide which team captain will elect to punt the football deep into the opponent's territory where the defensive unit makes a stand or to receive the football deep in home territory where the offensive unit then carries the values symbolized by its uprights toward the goal post at the opposite end of the field to score a touchdown. Both *Uncle Tom's Cabin* and *Enemy of the State* broach the topic of national security, setting individual right to privacy against the people's right to freedom of information.

Political shadowing of private citizens in Scott's star-studded film *Enemy of the State* counterpoints Stowe's portrayal of Negro emancipation in *Uncle Tom's Cabin*. Indeed, eavesdropping is an overlooked motif in *Uncle Tom's Cabin*. An instance of overhearing occurs early in the novel when Eliza Harris, a black maidservant, happens to pass in the hallway of the Kentucky mansion and overhears her master, Mr. Arthur Shelby, her mistress Emily Shelby's husband, negotiating a transfer of ownership for quick sale of Eliza Harris's five-year-old son to Mr. Haley, a prominent Louisiana slave trader: "Now, it had so happened that, in approaching the door, Eliza had caught enough of the conversation to know that a trader was making offers to her master for somebody" (Stowe 15). Presently, Mrs. Shelby, in a sincere effort to convince Eliza Harris that Mr. Shelby would never sell little Harry to a Southern slave trader, kindly admonishes Eliza Harris, scolding, "don't go listening at doors any more'" (Stowe 16). While *Uncle Tom's Cabin* focuses primarily on portraying Negro slaves' historic quest for freedom, *Enemy of the State* evokes African-American resilience, subtly incorporating uniquely-mounted runaway slave motifs into the political intrigue. In repositioning Stowe's antebellum Negroes George and Eliza Harris as affluent husband-and-wife attorneys Robert and Carla Dean, Scott's film anticipates Barack and Michelle Obama as the first African-American President and First Lady (2008-2016). While *Uncle Tom's Cabin* marks a revolutionary turning-point in fathoming civil rights as an all-inclusive defining principle of democracy, *Enemy of the State* dramatizes African perspectives, illuminating Middle Passage rupture, antebellum reverberation, and African-American redemption.

Both Stowe and Scott display intuitive feeling for black culture, which took root and thrived in America for more than five hundred years, notably traditional Nigeria-Yoruba-Land's theological belief in Esu-Elegbara's power. Christianity complements ancient Yoruba theology, instituted before 6000

BC. In Yoruba cosmology, Esu-Elegbara is a multifaceted divinity respected for anthropocentric characteristics, particularly capricious unpredictability. Pervasively and dynamically, Esu-Elegbara invigorates "public opinion," which is "that protean force by which complex aggregations of public attitude are understood to assert political leverage" (Mallios 721). Esu-Elegbara works invisibly, upwelling at gateways and crossings, carrying authority in the workings of American democracy, forming a wellspring of African-American advancement catalyzed by Stowe's grassroots depiction of a defining moment in the revolutionary turn toward Thirteenth Amendment abolition (1865). Reconstructing Stowe's anti-slavery novel, Scott's sophisticated film shows Esu-Elegbara-inspired power directing the outcome of a contemporary Legree's abuses.

Ostensibly, *Enemy of the State* is a politically-engaged parody of the way illegal use of high technology equipment and *quid pro quo* bribery by governmental officials for tyrannical control of Congress instigate subversive censorship, illegal surveillance practices, and widespread corruption. *Enemy of the State* depicts this naïve African-American barrister who inadvertently enters the crossfire between a corrupt security department head and a grass roots whistle blower. Two unrelated yet crisscrossing plots involving high-level white collar corruption and underworld activities in a mobster milieu erupt in a concluding scene of violence that turns a family restaurant into a war zone. *Enemy of the State* is a mordantly satirical anti-war film that obliquely and ironically suggests that the battlefield is a killing field that has gotten disconnected from the political issues that initially started the war.

Intriguingly, Scott's film builds momentum as politically-motivated violence converges hauntingly with antebellum racial violence and intersects with illustrative representations of racial inequality in Stowe's novel. *Enemy of the State*'s portrayal of Reynolds and his henchmen symbolically parallels Stowe's depiction of slave trader Haley and Northerner slave-owner Legree in *Uncle Tom's Cabin*. Overzealous politician Reynolds is a proponent of violating Americans' rights to privacy in the name of national security. Ironically, Reynolds is a cover-up artist bent on confiscating a birdwatcher's video-diskette catching Reynolds's assailants in the act of murdering in broad daylight Congressman Philip Hammersley [Jason Robards]. Having asserted his intention to defend the importance of creating more manufacturing jobs, Hammersley repeatedly refuses to acquiesce to Reynolds's demands that he vote for the Telecommunications Security and Privacy Act. Not recognizing Reynolds as a monomaniacal rogue, Hammersley offhandedly states his opposition while blithely exercising his golden retriever at Loch Raven Reservoir. Dean is an outsider to, yet a victim of, America's corporate-style politics. Dean is well-educated with highly-specialized knowledge of the right to remain silent, which saves his life in the end. Nonetheless, his non-technological orientation coincides with Negro slaves'

lack of education. Stephanie Deutsch observes, "Of all the myriad depriva-
tions imposed by slavery, the banning of education was arguably the most
devastating" (10). Fittingly, Dean's lack of interest in high-tech creates an
appearance of naïve ignorance accentuated by flashpoints of picaresque rog-
uishness akin to multilingual trickster spirit Esu-Elegbara. Reflecting Esu-
Elegbara's child-like unpredictability, Dean's son, Eric [Jascha Washington],
mistakes the evidentiary video-diskette for an early Christmas gift and unknowingly foils Reynolds's efforts to confiscate it from Dean.

While *Uncle Tom's Cabin* deepens archetypal representation of Negro
slaves' plight, revealing the benevolence of financially strapped slaveholders
Emily and Arthur Shelby, *Enemy of the State* enriches depiction of political
corruption undermining democratic freedoms, analogizing loss of all
American citizens' privacy rights to Negro slaves' loss of freedom. Instead
of rushing to judgment of events surrounding the 1850 Fugitive Slave Act,
Stowe and Scott evoke moral ambiguities in politically-controversial occurrences, artistically re-shaping catastrophic scenarios portraying national di-
lemmas into examinations of America's moral fiber. Dean's traumatic
retrogression to naïve ignorance and atavistic association with the institution
of slavery reincarnates George Harris's appropriating the American right to
defend oneself, countermanding Uncle Tom's Christian practice of "turning
the other cheek" (Matthew 5:38), which is traceable to African theology's
"African heart" concept of merciful forgiveness.[4] Uncle Tom typifies suffering servants stalwartly obedient to their masters. John R. Adams asserts,
Uncle Tom "preferred slavery and martyrdom to dishonorable flight" (32).
Enemy of the State portrays Dean as a neoteric George Harris re-embodied as
a modernistic personification of Esu-Elegbara. At first, Dean incarnates a
modern-day Uncle Tom compliant with the white Anglo Saxon Protestant
lifestyle, but his momentary contact with Zavitz, who has privileged knowledge—legally valid proof that Reynolds broke God's Sixth Commandment
to Moses in Holy Scripture, "Thou shalt not kill" (Exodus 20:13), suggests
Zavitz's and Dean's symbolic reclassification as archetypal Runaway Slaves
hotly pursued by trickster Reynolds, an avatar of Loki.

Thomas Brian Reynolds, the Dean family's adversary, reincarnates slaver
Haley, who is a "man of leather,—a man alive to nothing but trade and
profit,—cool, and unhesitating, and unrelenting, as death and the grave"
(Stowe 50). Carla and Robert Dean's son, Eric Dean, reincarnates Eliza and
George Harris's son, Harry Harris, who is "handsome, and smart, and bright"
(Stowe 27). Brilliant former NSA communications expert Edward "Brill"
Lyle [Gene Hackman] reincarnates reformed slave-hunter Tom Loker. As
runaway slave George Harris, blocked from escape to Canada, shoots Tom
Loker, then helps rescuers, some Quakers in the vicinity, to give wounded
slave-hunter Tom Loker medical aid, so, too, Robert Clayton Dean, who was
hired by bullied union workers, enables Brill, a recluse ensconced in a con-

demned building rigged with security cameras and demolition fuses, to re-
coup his confidence to perform his pre-retirement job and produce hi-tech
handiwork, giving go-between Rachel Banks [Lisa Bonet] a video-cassette
that shows Italian-American mafia boss Paulie Pintero [Tom Sizemore] violating his parole by hobnobbing with union management.

Enemy of the State begins with a scene reminiscent of Stowe's Chapter
XL "The Martyr" where Uncle Tom's life ends violently. Similar to *Uncle
Tom's Cabin's* account of brutality when Legree "smote his victim [Uncle
Tom] to the ground" (538), *Enemy of the State's* establishing-shot of the
assassination demonstrates the necessity of righting wrongful action through
exposing its perpetrators. The plot pits Reynolds against Philip Hammersley;
in the subplot, the firm of Silverberg and Blake Attorneys-at-Law assigns
African-American hero Robert Clayton Dean, an experienced labor lawyer,
to counsel beleaguered mafia godfather Paulie Pintero. *Enemy of the State's*
focus on two men, one a criminally corrupt white G-man, the other a prosperous African-American white-collar professional, suggests African-
Americans' socioeconomic progress 165 years after British Parliament's
Emancipation Bill, 140 years after Lincoln's Emancipation Proclamation,
and 34 years after the Civil Rights Act of 1964, the latter catalyzed by
assassination of Irish-American Catholic President John Kennedy in 1963.
Progress in legally provisioning minorities by outlawing discriminatory practices contrasts sharply to subversion of democratic principles by a corrupt
government official and his aides. Comparable to antebellum slaveholders
whose discriminatory acts of violence and civil rights violations were sanctioned by the 1850 Fugitive Slave Law, Reynolds clandestinely exploits legally-sanctioned telecommunications industry tools, including wire taps, hidden cameras, and satellite-driven tracking devices, to cover-up politically-
motivated criminal acts of aggression.

Similarly to *Uncle Tom's Cabin*, Scott's *Enemy of the State* suggests
erroneous thinking and character flaws are a root cause for legalization of
unfair treatment that travesties justice. Human frailty spawns and feeds mob
mentality, lawlessness, and political corruption. *Enemy of the State* illustrates
the insidious and sinister modus operandi of wrongheadedness juxtaposed
with Esu-Elegbara's restorative wiliness when Dean inadvertently comes
into possession of video-diskette evidence that incriminates Reynolds, showing his felonious attack against a senator who refuses to coerce colleagues.
Ultimately, archetypal African-American Dean is heroic in the line of
George Harris and Frederick Douglass (1818-1895). Ellen Moers asserts that
Stowe modeled George, who is "an intellectual, a radical, and a leader . . . a
hired-out slave employed at a skilled trade," on her reading of *Narrative of
the Life of Frederick Douglass* (15). Hired out by slave-master Harris to
work in "a bagging factory," George showed "adroitness and ingenuity
[which] caused him to be considered the first hand in the place," and he

"invented a machine," which "displayed quite as much mechanical genius as Whitney's cotton gin" (Stowe 19). Cowed by George's genius and by the adulation of George's white co-workers and employer, Mr. Wilson, Harris terminates George and takes him home, where Harris's son, Tom, flogs George and drowns his dog, Carlo, a gift from Eliza Harris. George Harris confides to Eliza Harris his anger, bitterness at being forced to haul things like "a dray-horse," and plan to escape to Canada (Stowe 25-26). Harris is afflicted by negative *persistence of vision*, his feeling of intimidation exacerbated by his mental image of George as a strong black slave, but, at the same time, a man whom antebellum American society constructs as inferior. Incisively, Stowe portrays Harris as a cruel master caught in the act of maintaining a socially-constructed model that molds George into a Runaway Slave. Later, in a Kentucky tavern, Wilson diplomatically points out to George, traveling *in cognito* as Mr. Butler, that his plan to join the Runaway Slave movement is nonviolent, justifiable, but unlawful:

> Mr. Wilson, a good-natured but extremely fidgety and cautious old gentleman, ambled up and down the room, appearing, as John Bunyan hath it, "much tumbled up and down in his mind," and divided between his wish to help George, and a certain confused notion of maintaining law and order; so, as he shambled about, he delivered himself as follows: "Well, George, I s'pose you're running away—leaving your lawful master, George—(I don't wonder at it)—at the same time, I'm sorry, George,—yes, decidedly—I think I must say that, George—it's my duty to tell you so." (Stowe 145)

Nevertheless, Stowe's mouthpiece, Wilson is a Christian who reveals empathetic understanding of West African Vodun Yoruba Godhead Olodumare. When George asks if there is a God for Negro slaves, Wilson says, "clouds and darkness are around him, but righteousness and judgment are the habitation of his throne. There's a *God*, George,—believe it; trust in Him" (153).

As slaver Harris despotically distributes dead-or-alive runaway slave wanted posters against George Harris, so, too, Thomas Brian Reynolds stalks Jewish-American Daniel Leon Zavitz and African-American Robert Clayton Dean. When Daniel Leon Zavitz hurriedly plants the tape of the murder, the close-up of his hand slipping the video-diskette into his fellow Georgetown University graduate's shopping bag evokes an associative transference of meaning. Unambiguously, the video-diskette is a thing, i.e., a piece of property that carries evidentiary proof of Thomas Brian Reynolds's homicidal guilt, which Daniel Leon Zavitz gives to Robert Clayton Dean, who does not know that he now possesses evidence of a murder. At this moment, African-American attorney Robert Clayton Dean unknowingly and unintentionally becomes a player in the assassination cover-up. While this plot complication enhances *Enemy of the State*'s intrigue, the status of protagonist Robert Clayton Dean suffers an anachronistic setback because the role he plays reduces him to being merely a thing. Robert Clayton Dean unknowingly becomes a pawn in a larger scenario, similarly to the way Eliza Harris and her family are Negro slaves marginalized, their personhood destroyed by their socioeconomically constructed role as marketable merchandise in the form of transatlantic cargo, Negro slaves who bore the burden of carrying America's Cotton Empire on their shoulders.

Nonetheless, Tony Scott depicts Daniel Leon Zavitz and Robert Clayton Dean as archetypal Olympic torch bearers when the former passes the videodiskette to the latter in a virtual relay race to redeem justice by shining the light on truth, demonstrating sympathetic understanding of the ethical position to which Stowe gives artistic expression in *Uncle Tom's Cabin.* In her Preface, Harriet Beecher Stowe clearly enunciates her intention not to portray all black slaves but an outstanding man whose conversion to Christianity is authentic. Daughter of a Christian minister, Stowe envisions a time in the future when liberated black slaves will be free to return to Africa to evangelize in the homeland of their forebears. Stowe sees her role as a Christian-American writer as a feminist embodiment of Moses leading Hebrew slaves across the Red Sea to their homeland Israel:

> When an enlightened and Christianized community shall have on the shores of Africa, laws, language and literature, drawn from among us, may then the scenes of the house of bondage be to them like the remembrance of Egypt to the Israelite,—a motive of thankfulness to Him who hath redeemed them! For, while politicians contend, and men are swerved this way and that by conflicting tides of interest and passion, the great cause of human liberty is in the hands of [Christ]. (Stowe 3)

Tony Scott's political thriller *Enemy of the State* evokes the redemptive power not only of Christ but also the decisive input of gatekeeper Esu-Elegbara. Tony Scott creates a multidimensional Runaway Slave variant that stops short of situation comedy in the chase scenes to convey the spirit Harriet Beecher Stowe invokes in her anti-slavery novel depicting Uncle Tom as a black Christian slave who models the Biblical Suffering Servant at the crossroads where life intersects with death.

Stowe suggests that the subtitle *Life among the Lowly* refers both to socioeconomically oppressed black people and to hypocritical Christians who buy and sell fellow human beings, exemplifying the basest precincts of the human race. Stowe emphasizes her concern to show contrasts between the Christian soul of black slave Uncle Tom and Un-Christian misconduct of slaver Harris. Anthropological acumen strengthens her respect for Uncle Tom, whom she esteems as a prototypal model of humanity. In her Preface, she writes,

Unhappy Africa at last is remembered; Africa, who began the race of civilization and human progress in the dim, gray dawn of early time, but who, for
centuries, has lain bound and bleeding at the foot of civilized and Christianized
humanity, imploring compassion in vain (Stowe 2).

In *Enemy of the State,* martyred Jewish-American Daniel Leon Zavitz re-
embodies Lucy's feisty faith in God. Distraught young mother Lucy escapes
Haley's clutches by jumping overboard into the Mississippi River during
passage on *La Belle Rivière* steamboat, which symbolizes ships carrying
West African slaves north to Britain and west to the Americas and Caribbean
archipelago, whereupon Haley "sat discontentedly down, with his little ac-
count-book, and put down the missing body and soul under the head of
losses!" (Stowe 174). Daniel Leon Zavitz traverses an urban labyrinth, grabs
a bicycle, clutching the murder video-diskette as he gyrates along Washington's thoroughfares, killed while attempting to escape from Reynolds's
henchmen, who view Philip Hammersley and Daniel Leon Zavitz as expend-
able things that block their agenda to violate freedom and liberty in the name
of national security.

Not only remarkable thematic parallels but mirroring-reversals align *Enemy of the State* with *Uncle Tom's Cabin.* Crossroads imagery permeates their
plot designs and character depictions. Intersections coincide with radical plot
shifts precipitating crisis moments of defiance, fear, love, and bravery insti-
gating headlong actions prompted by covert eavesdropping opportunities.
Predictably, benevolent slave owner Emily Shelby protests to her husband,
Arthur, after he confesses to her that he made a deal to sell Uncle Tom to
slave-trader Haley. Highlighting covert information procurement's centrality
in a free democratic society, Stowe portrays Eliza Harris overhearing, from
her hiding-place in a closet, the Shelbys' argument over sale of Uncle Tom
and little Harry Harris to Haley: "With her ear pressed close against the crack
of the door, she had lost not a word of the conversation," which enables her
to flee with Harry (Stowe 50). Likewise, Phinias Fletcher overhears slave-
hunters scheming to send George Harris back to Kentucky, transport Eliza
Harris to New Orleans for sale to a plantation owner, return their small child
to Haley, and take Jim Selden and his mother back to their masters in Kentucky. Within a legal framework, *Enemy of the State* mirrors, i.e., presents a
reversed picture of, the situation in *Uncle Tom's Cabin.* Despite his federal
agent status, Thomas Brian Reynolds unlawfully eliminates Philip Hammersley. In contrast, slave-holders loath Haley, but his commercial enterprise is
legal. Stowe emphasizes Haley's sacrilegious moral laxity: "George stood
with clenched hands and glowing eyes, and looking as any other man might
look, whose wife was to be sold at auction, and son sent to a trader, all under
the shelter of a Christian nation's laws" (247). The bounty hunters rebuke the
Quakers who shelter George Harris: "You see, we're officers of justice.

We've got the law on our side, and the power" (Stowe 258). The bounty hunters' repression parallels Reynolds's homicidal arrogance in *Enemy of the State*.

Thomas Brian Reynolds's felonious killing of Philip Hammersley parallels callous and profligate treatment of antebellum whites. The 1850 Fugitive Slave Law sanctioned severe punishment inflicted on white Americans found to be giving shelter to runaway Negroes. Thomas Brian Reynolds, an anarchical extremist, adopts a Machiavellian "might makes right" political philosophy, deceiving himself into believing he has a national security concern to protect the State (America) by allocating to his agency an absolute right to supersede citizens' rights to privacy and impose unlimited wiretapping, search and seizure, and arbitrary police-state action against private citizens without obtaining bench warrants or other legal documentation adjudicated under federal statutes. Tony Scott depicts Thomas Brian Reynolds as a counterpart to archetypal anti-abolitionist Simon Legree. At the heart of Tony Scott's *Enemy of the State*, Thomas Brian Reynolds literally strips black American citizen Dean of his social and economic status. Harriet Beecher Stowe's Chapter XXXI "The Middle Passage" depicts dehumanization symbolically when Simon Legree denudes Uncle Tom, who "had been attired for sale in his best broadcloth suit, with well-starched linen and shining boots," and orders Uncle Tom to don "old pantaloons" and a "dilapidated coat" and "coarse, stout shoes" and confiscates "Tom's Methodist hymnbook" because, Simon Legree says, "*I'm* your church now!" (440-41).

Enemy of the State achieves a brilliant structural design that harmonizes philosophically with the subtle allusions to West African Vodun cosmological theology. This critically acclaimed feature film turns upon the thematic axis of the metamorphosis of a prominent Washington, D.C. attorney retrogressively back to being a slave, indeed a runaway slave. This thematic axis combines pleasingly with the machinations of the Vodun divinity Esu-Elegbara. Analogous to West Europeans faithful for centuries to hierarchical Roman Catholicism, West African Vodun and Yoruba cosmology adherents cleave strongly and steadfastly to monotheist[5] faith in demi-divinities governing global spheres of influence. Significant numbers of African-Americans are descendants of Middle Passage survivors who honor traditional West African Vodun and Yoruba theological beliefs and practices. Chief among these religious survivals is conscious and unconscious belief in the ideals of Esu-Elegbara, guardian of crossroads and gateways associated with turning points and rites of passage. Esu-Elegbara's distinctive worldly quality is death-defying skill in handling complicated states of affairs. Permeating *Enemy of the State*'s structural design is this Esu-Elegbara motif, which catapults Dean into the thick of the intrigue yet also keeps him from being crushed by it. *Enemy of the State*'s climactic episode employs dramatic irony to enhance Dean's adept demonstration of African-American intelligence. In the climactic gunfight between Thomas Brian Reynolds and Paulie Pintero, Robert Clayton Dean epitomizes Esu-Elegbara as the multi-ethnic NSA political plot and Italian-American mafia subplot intersect with the esoteric Yoruba Esu-Elegbara and Norse Loki motif. Dean gets entangled in the machinations of a trio of ruthless killers, dishonorably-discharged U.S. Marines who make illegal use of their time and equipment as NSA employees. His connection to this clandestine activity forms a chain of happenstance occurrences.

His metamorphosis from prosperous attorney to fugitive slave begins at Ruby's Shop, where fleeing Daniel Leon Zavitz stows the assassination video-diskette in Robert Clayton Dean's shopping bag containing Christmas gifts for Carla Dean and Eric Dean. Similarly to slave trader Haley's tyrannical abuse of Uncle Tom, Thomas Brian Reynolds harasses and torments Robert Clayton Dean wielding high-tech surveillance devices as a slave-master's whip. Soon, Robert Clayton Dean loses his household possessions, credit accounts, and clothing. Meanwhile, he regains his African identity, transforming him into a symbolic Esu-Elegbara. Obliquely, *Enemy of the State* reveals Dean's cultural heritage rooted historically in Yoruba theology. Robert Clayton Dean alights ashore from the *Baltimore Patriot*, emblematizing a slave ship, whereupon he encounters Yellow Cab driver ersatz Brill [Gabriel Byrne], who symbolically baptizes Robert Clayton Dean as a transmigrated African slave whose cell-phone, pager, watch, shoes, pants, and pen must be *debugged* (double-entendre: insects and parasitic tracking devices). This Brill impersonator orders Robert Clayton Dean to remove his shoe for debugging, echoing Simon Legree ordering Uncle Tom to "Stand up . . . Take off that stock . . . Take off your boots" (Stowe 44). When Reynolds's goons ransack the Dean family's residence hunting for the incriminating video-diskette, this raid parallels Simon Legree's selling Uncle Tom's "very neat and abundant wardrobe" to Red River boat crewmen and auctioning Uncle Tom's trunk. After the Deans lose everything, Edward "Brill" Lyle, who is tougher than political puppeteer Thomas Brian Reynolds, contrapuntally reincarnates Simon Legree:

> Mr. Legree, having refitted Tom's handcuffs, proceeded deliberately to investigate the contents of his pockets. He drew out a silk handkerchief, and put it into his own pocket. Several little trifles, which Tom had treasured, chiefly because they had amused Eva he looked upon with a contemptuous grunt, and tossed them over his shoulder into the river (Stowe 440-41).

Reconstructing Simon Legree's stripping Uncle Tom, Brill detains Robert Clayton Dean in a skyscraper elevator, ordering him to remove his shoe and pants, then confiscates Dean's pen, and on the rooftop tells Robert Clayton Dean to toss his watch (a gift from Carla Dean). This symbolic drama contrapuntally mirrors slave-master Simon Legree's stripping Uncle Tom, asserting Brill's intent to block Thomas Brian Reynolds's criminally-motivated intrusion into every facet of Robert Clayton Dean's life.

Enemy of the State parodies the slave trade ambiance. In a pastiche of the archetypal native African seized by slave traders in Africa and America, Robert Clayton Dean is taken unawares. Initially, Dean's success indicates virtual obliteration of socioeconomic color lines that sharply set slave classes apart from affluent mercantile classes. Comically-underscored, yet tragically-accentuated, Robert Clayton Dean's reversal of fortune evokes contraventions the institution of slavery imposed on the institution of the family. By chance, Robert Clayton Dean pauses at Ruby's ladies' lingerie shop window display and lightheartedly decides to buy Christmas gifts for Carla Dean. Ignoring attractive white models scantily clad in black brassieres and garter belts, Robert Clayton Dean replies to the greeter's "See anything you like?" with an ethically-charged rejoinder ("I'm married!"), evoking parallels between Ruby's Shop and the slave-market auction block that separates husbands from their wives. Scott's *Enemy of the State* reconstructs *Uncle Tom's Cabin*'s Chapter XXX "The Slave Warehouse" where "men have learned the art of sinning expertly and genteelly, so as not to shock the eyes and senses of respectable society. Human property . . . [comes] to sale sleek, and strong, and shining . . . Outside . . . rows of men and women stand there as a sign of the property sold within" (Stowe 426). Tony Scott reconstructs Harriet Beecher Stowe's dramatization of slavery's impact on marriage. This antebellum parallel enhances *Enemy of the State*'s in-depth depiction of America's state of mind during the epoch between the 1964 Civil Rights Act and recent affirmations of Fourth Amendment prohibitions against governmental surveillance, stalking, search and seizure of private citizens. *Enemy of the State* dovetails concern for racial minorities whose civil rights lag behind Anglo-Saxon Protestant males' rights with America's growing concern about threats that endanger national security at home and abroad. Evocatively, *Enemy of the State* shows that racism is a real threat to national security. Scott creates suspense utilizing extended dramatic irony to portray the depths of Robert Clayton Dean's dilemma. Robert Clayton Dean is shocked by Daniel Leon Zavitz's untimely death, and his unawareness of the homicide video-diskette is situational. His African cultural heritage enables him to rise slowly to the occasion, incessantly forced to defend and protect his democratic freedoms using improvisatory tactics and spur-of-the-moment stratagems.

As the plot unfolds, a salient pattern of Fugitive Slave imagery emerges in sequences extending from Daniel Leon Zavitz as archetypal Runaway Slave traversing rooftops and colliding fatally with a fire engine to Dean outrunning assassination-cover-up specialists in a hotel where Dean's stripping is redolent of nineteenth-century vaudeville popularized in America, England,

and China. Robert Clayton Dean startles a Chinese man and his wife, the Wu couple [Nancy Yee and Albert Wong], in their hotel room, suddenly appearing, a well-dressed gentleman who gains entry, entertainingly impersonating a quality-assurance technician. When Dean removes his clothing to rid himself of tracking devices, he tickles Mrs. Wu's fancy but Mr. Wu does not enjoy the striptease. Then, Robert Clayton Dean reprises George Harris's fire-and-brimstone passion when, trapped in a linen closet, he mobilizes the fire department. Tony Scott obtrusively and unmistakably reenacts Runaway Slave escapism when Robert Clayton Dean exits an ambulance, strides perilously into traffic-congested intersections, and miraculously eludes capture in a freeway tunnel. During a lull in the video-diskette chase, Dean momentarily dodges his pursuers and trysts with his wife, Carla Dean [Regina King], in the Dean family's carport. Carla Dean's tense body language and welcoming embrace are reminiscent of Eliza Harris's mood and greeting to George Harris in *Uncle Tom's Cabin*: "Eliza stood in the verandah, rather dejectedly looking after [Mrs. Shelby's] retreating carriage, when a hand was laid on her shoulder. She turned and a bright smile lighted up her fine eyes. 'George, is it you? How you frightened me! Well; I am so glad you's come!'" (Stowe 23).

Accentuating slavery-imposed persistence of vision, Robert Clayton Dean's pet dog and Brill's pet cat are totemic symbols. *Uncle Tom's Cabin* metaphorically compares slaves to puppies in Haley's sales pitch for black infants: "They is raised as easy as any kind of critter there is going; they an't a bit more trouble than pups" (168). In *Enemy of the State*, white Pomeranian Porsche symbolizes disruptive rerouting when he knocks over a glass, spilling red wine on Dean's legal documents, signaling Dean's Christ-like martyrdom and anachronistic metamorphosis from attorney to slave. Later, Thomas Brian Reynolds's goons spray terror-stricken Porsche green, a color that suggests Haley's venality and Reynolds's covetousness. Likewise, Brill resembles "bull-dog" Tom Loker, whose companion is "lithe and catlike" Marks, a predatory antebellum lawyer who "[pokes] his sharp nose and chin" into lucrative slave swaps and captures (Stowe 86, 88). Having rigged his hideaway with explosives, Brill, who opposes Reynolds's criminal assassination cover-up, only lets Robert Clayton Dean into his getaway vehicle after he sees his cat, Babe, cradled in Dean's arms. His hostility is precipitated by Dean's disobedience of his orders not to telephone anybody. Brill's hesitation before opening the car door and the ensuing in-your-face violent confrontation over a rifle suggests white master and black slave intersecting, eyes locked in a master-slave gaze.

The climactic gunfight scene in *Enemy of the State* suggests Esu-Elegbara's political power surge as Dean utilizes an African-American "faculty" described by Sam in *Uncle Tom's Cabin*. Black Sam attributes to Negroes "a habit of bobservation" that "makes all the difference" in enabling them to respond quickly and intuitively in an emergency. Black Sam observed that slave-owner Mrs. Shelby wanted Eliza Harris to escape and he delayed Haley's pursuit because, he says, "Didn't I see which way the wind blew dis yer mornin'? Didn't I see what Missis wanted, though she never let on? Dan ar's bobservation, Andy. I 'spects it's what you may call a faculty. Faculties is different in different peoples, but cultivation of 'em goes a great way" (67). This "bobservation" trait differentiates Stowe's ethnologically verisimilitudinous depiction of Sam from Huck Finn's naïve description of Jim, which is liable to promote *pernicious persistence of vision*. Huck Finn bases his differentiation of a white man from a black man on his belief that only the latter would always choose to run away. Huck tells Jim, *"now,* old Jim, you're a free man *again,* and I bet you won't ever be a slave no more" (Twain 283). Insightfully and wittily, Jim praises Tom Sawyer and Huck Finn's "beautiful" planning and execution of Jim's escape, emphasizing that *"nobody"* else could have devised "a plan" any more "mixed-up" and "splendid" (283). Consternation strikes the happy trio when Tom Sawyer yelps in pain from a bullet wound to his leg, yet insists on moving ahead with the escape plan. Jim communes with Huck, who tells Jim to speak his mind. Jim responds rhetorically: if Tom were the one being set free and one of his liberators were shot, would Tom override the need for a doctor? Jim is certain that Tom would choose calling a doctor before being set free. Jim states he will not take another step toward freedom until Huck Finn summons a doctor to care for Tom Sawyer's wound. Upon hearing Jim's summation, Huck Finn, an unreliable first-person narrator, asserts, "I knowed he was white inside, and I reckoned he'd say what he did say—so it was all right now, and I told Tom I was agoing for a doctor" (Twain 284). But Huck Finn fails to recognize in Jim a quality similar to Sam's profound insights into the human heart. Huck Finn praises Jim for being white on the inside, black on the outside, attributing Jim's caring concern, not to Jim's blackness but to whiteness. Naïve narrator Huck Finn fails to see that Jim's goodness is an expression of blackness. Erroneously believing he pays Jim a compliment, Huck Finn fails to see his racially-motivated prejudicial attitude to Jim.

Although Robert Clayton Dean loses many "battles," his African heritage, epitomized in Stowe's Sam, enables him to analyze Reynolds's and Pintero's psychological mindsets, apply that analysis to the endgame, and then opt out of the situation. Activating his ability to manipulate variables then passively withdraw, he transforms his disadvantage as an atavistic avatar of the Middle Passage African and antebellum Runaway Slave into strength, successfully using his verbal skills in rhetorical persuasion to gain the cooperation and confidence of Pintero, Rachel, Brill, Eric, and even Reynolds. An emblem of tragic-comic Esu-Elegbara, Dean negotiates an agreement with Reynolds, simulates "black magic" making two videotapes appear as one, outmaneuvering Reynolds and Pintero, then waits beneath a table while bullets fly.

Dean improvises a role reversal, gaining the upper hand over radicalized maverick Thomas Brian Reynolds, a pivotal figure that bridges Tony Scott's twenty-first century and Civil War scenarios.

Tony Scott in *Enemy of the State* evokes the Civil War battle he and Ridley Scott vividly reenact in their film *Gettysburg*, which documents the defeat of the Confederate army under General Robert E. Lee's command by the Union army led by Major General George Meade under President Lincoln's direct command. Major General John Reynolds, headstrong Commander of the First Corps, was relieved of duty after he was

> summoned to the White House by the President after the battle of Chancellorsville, where they talked late into the night of June 2 [1863]. Lincoln had felt him out about assuming the command . . . and *Reynolds had stipulated that he would accept only if allowed untrammeled authority to direct the army's movements, i.e., if he were free of orders* from [Henry W.] Halleck. (Tucker 73; my italics)

The demise of Thomas Brian Reynolds in *Enemy of the State* echoes the slapdash leadership and death of Major General John F. Reynolds during the Civil War:

> Near the summit of McPherson's Ridge, Reynolds was directing the two regiments in the enveloping movement. He was mounted on his black horse and wore the major general's shoulder straps. *Carelessly exposing himself and obviously an officer of high rank*, he at once drew the fire of [Confederate Brigadier General James J.] Archer's skirmishers, who had crossed Willoughby Run and worked their way up the wooded hillside. *Reynolds, expecting support, had turned in the saddle to look toward the crest of the ridge behind him. It was 10:15 A.M. He was struck in the back of the neck by* . . . a marksman from a tree on the bank of the stream. (Tucker 110-111; my italics)

Scott's depiction of *Enemy of the State*'s endgame parallels missed signals and battlefield command miscommunications at Gettysburg.

The barrage of gunfire in *Enemy of the State*'s concluding sequence constitutes a concatenation of violence that metonymically evokes the "largest artillery bombardment in the Western Hemisphere" (Scott and Scott, *Gettysburg*). On July 3, 1863, the Union army of nearly 100,000 soldiers wearing blue uniforms put one hundred state-of-the-art Napoleon cannons into defensive formation against Confederate artillery that formed a line two miles long. Meade tricked the Rebel field command into surmising that sudden silence meant the ammunition arsenal was exhausted (Scott and Scott *Gettysburg*). The Rebel troops could not withdraw even though Brigadier General Pendleton had removed Napoleon cannons Colonel E.P. Alexander intended for the "indispensable function of shelling the Federal lines at the last minute before the Southern infantry struck" (Tucker 356). The Federal artillery com-

menced firing at 72,000 whooping Confederate foot soldiers armed with
muskets advancing as a massive column comprised of choleric Rebels clad in
homemade work clothes in the eighty-seven degree heat (Scott and Scott,
Gettysburg). The sound of rapidly-fired blasts of mortar igniting monstrous
balls of powder exploding on contact, leaving 23,000 killed, wounded, and
missing-in-action, was heard in Harrisburg, forty miles away.

Revitalizing Sam's spirit, Dean emulates African-American redemption
as a modern Esu-Elegbara and sidesteps the conflagration using African-
American "bobservation." The camera shot of Dean finding sanctuary under
a table suggests an evocative parallel with slaves who found asylum via the
Underground Railroad, which took 500,000 fugitive slaves from Virginia and
Maryland to Pennsylvania, New York, and Canada. One hundred fifty thousand Negro slaves enlisted in the Union army, as combat soldiers, stretcher
bearers (serving wounded Union and Confederate soldiers) and hospital
staffers assisting 20,000 women nurses (Scott and Scott, *Gettysburg*). Cham-
pioning African-American societal savoir-faire, knowledge of statutory laws,
and soul-integrity, Dean personifies Esu-Elegbara at a crossroads where
Thomas Brian Reynolds loses his life because he unwittingly bargains with
Paulie Pintero mistakenly believing Paulie Pintero has the assassination
video-diskette, while Paulie Pintero risks his life, vociferously defending his
right to the murder tape erroneously believing Thomas Brian Reynolds wants
the video-cassette showing Paulie Pintero socializing with underworld union
cronies. Rather than depicting these political cross-purposes as an allegory of
good against evil, *Enemy of the State*, while obliquely commenting on the
concept of consent of the governed in the *Declaration of Independence*,
invokes Esu-Elegbara's nimble-mindedness, which presides over intricacies
of meaning, existential trickiness at the core of America's democratic pluralism. As a republic, America, in becoming increasingly more democratically-
minded, has almost imperceptibly become more African.

Americans' willingness to accept decisions by majority vote perpetuates
Esu-Elegbara's spirited gatekeeping. Structurally, America's two-party political system is contingent on the people's faith in decision-making by electoral voting that constructs matrices' plotting points where multiple perspectives converge to document consensus and citizenry participation. Vitally a
geopolitical spiritual authority, Esu-Elegbara symbolizes friendship and
unity amidst enmity and dissension. On an international scale, Esu-Elegbara's power may be conceptualized as energizing and ethically infusing strate-
gic communications among global leaders. Significantly, the Federal Republic of Nigeria, Africa's largest black population (200,000,000), comprising
Yoruba[6] , Muslim, Christian, and Jewish communities, is one of the world's
best-run English-administered democratic nations.

By foregrounding morality and legality, conscience and consciousness,
Stowe, Twain, and Scott underscore the ripple effect of racism even though

individuals, not their race, are held to be responsible for their conduct. At the same time and with greater intensity, these humanistic artists suggest that all races, whether black, white, red, brown, yellow, or mixed race contribute to the political culture of America, which is as deep as it is wide. These artists suggest that pluralistic democracy depends for stability and viability on elusive phenomena personified by multilingual Yoruba intercessor, arbitrator, and mediator Esu-Elegbara. Esu-Elegbara and Loki, as black and white trickster figures, bridge mathematical probability outcomes and globally impact social, psychological, and political patterns of community and communication. In the European Union, German-born Valéry Giscard d'Estaing, President of France (1974-1981), stresses global perspicacity, observing that media and social networking are turning the world upside-down. World leaders are compelled to look up to the people (Interview). *Uncle Tom's Cabin* is Stowe's proclamation of solid triumph for the mind-soul in any body, regardless of class, creed, race or nation. Equality of individuals under the law seems a simple concept. Scott, Twain, and Scott show that history contains fallible models that impact our daily lives. Understanding the intricate complexity of democratic pluralism in the context of global culture smooths pathways toward lifting sociopolitical struggles to the high ground of language and discourse. Stowe, Twain, and Scott augment our understanding of historic roles black and white cultural contributions play in shaping pluralistic American democracy. Esu-Elegbara's multi-perspectival complexity is a crucial factor in assuring the effectiveness of democracy and of global cooperation in general. The volatile and elusive values osmotically instilled in America's and Nigeria's democratic, as well as in other nations' (e.g., Iran's Yoruba Sh'ia Islam theocratic), governments by Yoruba cosmology's Esu-Elegbara play a greater role than has hitherto been recognized as such. Global society's survival may depend on our collective knowledge of Africa-derived wisdom. To save our soul and our planet, Stowe, Twain, and Scott suggest that we all must learn to sing Africa.

Contemporary America continues to endure reverberations of the Fugitive Slave Act of 1850 traceable to the legally-sanctioned bloodcurdling practice of hunting down escaped slaves by the titillating use of bloodhounds, favoring the mercenary practice of treating human beings as commodities. Historically, the Fugitive Slave Law of 1850 was rooted in the Fugitive Slave Law of 1793, an Act of Congress reaffirming the Fugitive slave Clause in the United States Constitution, which guaranteed the right of slave-owners to pursue and seize runaway slaves. On December 6, 1865, the Thirteenth Amendment to the United States Constitution abolished slavery, except as a valid punishment, leaving a residue of stereotypical images to "govern."

NOTES

1. The "first documented instance" of "the presence of Africans in [New England]" was in Jamestown in 1619, predating "the arrival of the Pilgrims by one year"; "by 1807, 400,000 native-born Africans had been brought to America" (Gioia 7).
2. "[Esu-Elegbara], the trickster of the West African Dahomeans and Yorubans" (Herskovits 190). Nigeria-Yoruba Land respects Esu-Elegbara's sociopolitical cogency.
3. African-American jazz musicians performed in London and throughout Europe in the early 1930s, inspiring imitators and hybridized jazz forms (Gioia 170-71).
4. Trinyan Mariano discusses "mercy" as a post-Reconstruction legal term.
5. Yoruba theological Godhead is Olodumare, diarchically associated with Olorun, supreme creator and ruler of Heaven.
6. Yoruba cosmology's compatibility with Christianity enabled Negro slaves to survive. Simon Gikandi attributes Yoruba's enduring linguistic vitality to Yoruba translation of the Bible by Samuel Ajayi Crowther (1809-1891) "the first African bishop of the Niger" and to "creativity opened up by technologies of writing and by electronic media" (12-13).

WORKS CITED

Adams, John R. *Harriet Beecher Stowe*. Boston: Twayne, 1989.
Ammons, Elizabeth, and Susan Belasco. Introduction. *Approaches to Teaching Stowe's Uncle Tom's Cabin*. New York: Modern Language Association of America, 2000. 1-4.
Cobley, Paul. "The Paranoid Style in Narrative: The Anxiety of Storytelling After 9/11." *Narratologia: Intermediality and Storytelling*. Berlin, DEU: Walter de Gruyter, 2010. ProQuest ebrary. 24 June 2015. 99-121.
Deutsch, Stephanie. *You Need a Schoolhouse: Booker T. Washington, Julius Rosenwald, and the Building of Schools for the Segregated South*. Evanston: Northwestern University Press, 2011.
Enemy of the State. Directed by Tony Scott. Written by David Marconi. Costumes Designed by Marlene Stewart. Touchstone Pictures / Buena Vista, 1998. January 2, 2014. Television.
Gettysburg. Produced and directed by Tony Scott and Ridley Scott. History Channel, 2011. Television.
Gikandi, Simon. Editor's Column. "The Fragility of Languages." *PMLA* 130 (Jan. 2015): 9-14.
Gioia, Ted. *The History of Jazz*. New York: Oxford University Press, 1997.
Giscard d'Estaing, Valéry. Interview. Charlie Rose Show. Public Broadcasting System. New York. June 4, 2015. Television.
Glaser, Ben. "Folk Iambics: Prosody, Vestiges, and Sterling Brown's *Outline for the Study of the Poetry of American Negroes*." *PMLA* 129 (May 2014): 417-34.
Harris, Susan K. Introduction. *The Minister's Wooing*. By Harriet Beecher Stowe. New York: Penguin, 1999. vii-xxiii.
Hedrick, Joan. *Harriet Beecher Stowe: A Life*. New York: Oxford University Press, 1994.
Herskovits, Melville J. *Cultural Dynamics*. Abridged from *Cultural Anthropology*. 1947. New York: Knopf, 1964.
Herzog, Kristin. "*Uncle Tom's Cabin* and *Incidents in the Life of a Slave Girl*: The Issue of Violence." *Approaches to Teaching Stowe's Uncle Tom's Cabin*. Edited by Elizabeth Ammons and Susan Belasco. New York: Modern Language Association of America, 2000. 132-41.
The Holy Bible. Old and New Testaments. King James Version. New York: Books, c. 1951.
Hughes, Langston. "I, Too, Sing America." 1925. *The Collected Poems*. New York: Knopf, 2007. 46.
Kirkham, E. Bruce. *The Building of Uncle Tom's Cabin*. Knoxville: University of Tennessee Press, 1977.

Magny, Claude-Edmonde. *The Age of the American Novel: The Film Aesthetic of Fiction between the Two Wars.* [*L'Age du roman américain.* Paris, 1948]. Translated by Eleanor Hochman. New York: Ungar, 1972.

Mallios, Peter Lancelot. "Tragic Constitution: United States Democracy and Its Discontents." *PMLA* 129 (Oct. 2014): 708-726.

Mariano, Trinyan. "The Law of Torts and the Logic of Lynching in Charles Chestnutt's *The Marrow of Tradition.*" *PMLA* 128 (May 2013): 559-74.

Millward, David. "Obama warns of American legacy of racism." *The Telegraph.* 5 May 2015. 6:09 AM. British Standard Time. 5 May 2015. Web. 6 May 2015.

Moers, Ellen. *Harriet Beecher Stowe and American Literature.* Hartford: Stowe-Day Foundation, 1978.

Nicol, Abioseh. "The Meaning of Africa." *Africa Is Thunder and Wonder: Contemporary Voices from African Literature.* Ed. Barbara Nolen. New York: Scribner, 1972. 9-10. Rpt. of "The Continent That Lies Within Us." By Davidson [Aioseh] Nicol. *An Anthology of West African Verse.* Compiled by Olumbe Bassir. Ibadan, Nigeria: Ibadan University Press, 1957. 63-66.

"Remembering 'Top Gun' Director Tony Scott." *All Things Considered.* National Public Radio. 20 Aug. 2012. *Literature Resource Center.* Web. 5 May 2015.

Smith, Alexander McCall. *The No. 1 Ladies' Detective Agency.* Edinburgh, Scotland: Polygon, 1998; New York and Toronto: Random, Anchor, 2002.

Stowe, Harriet Beecher. *Uncle Tom's Cabin; or Life among the Lowly.* Cambridge: Harvard University Press, 2009.

Sturluson, Snorri. *The Prose Edda: Norse Mythology.* Translated by Jesse L. Byock. London and New York: Penguin, 2005.

Tucker, Glenn. *High Tide at Gettysburg: The Campaign in Pennsylvania.* Old Saybrook, CT: Konecky and Konecky, n.d.

Twain, Mark. *The Adventures of Huckleberry Finn.* London, 1884. New York and London: Sterling, 2006.

Chapter Two

Zora Neale Hurston

Africa Transported to America

Zora Neale Hurston (1891-1960) revolutionizes the American novel and enriches American culture by innovatively infusing *Their Eyes Were Watching God* (1937) with her deep-down knowledge of the ancient (9000 B.C) cosmology of West African Vodun, a theology that has been popularized and dubbed "voodoo," a Neo-African term. The Vodun religion takes its name from the Fon/Ewe word *vodun*, which means "spirit." West Africans formally inaugurated their worship of creation deity Damballah Ouedo in the fifth century B.C. in the ancient city of Yoruba at Oyo Temple. Hurston's narrative artistry penetrates to the heart of black consciousness by combining the spiritualism of West African theology with the Christian religious culture of African Americans, initially portraying in *Jonah's Gourd Vine* (1934) a mutually reinforcing interaction between native West African Vodun theology and Judeo-Christian scripture, then achieving another level of novelistic perfection in her representation of Janie Mae Crawford as an atavistic paragon of Vodun femininity as modeled by Ayida Ouedo, a Vodun *orisha*, or sky and heaven deity. Derek Collins and Daphne Lamothe suggest parallels between Janie Mae Crawford and Haitian Vodou(n) goddess of erotic love, Ezili Freda, and Edward M. Pavlic shows Esu-Elegba's influence. I widen the scope of findings in these excellent pioneering studies in challenging the supposition in *The Norton Anthology of African American Literature* that *Jonah's Gourd Vine*, was "impressive" as a first novel and "well received by both the critics and the public [but] prepared few readers for the book that was to follow" ("Zora Neale Hurston" 998). *Jonah's Gourd Vine* is a Vodun-Judeo-Christian American novel that is a prelude to *Their Eyes Were Watching God*, which is an exuberant African-American novel of life. But it is also a brilliant testimony to the Vodun ideal of religiously imbued high-spirited integrity that Janie Mae Crawford personifies. When she tells the story of her life to her best friend, Pheoby Watson, who in addition to being a confidante is a symbolic representative of the Southern Baptist parish of Eatonville, Florida, she recounts experiences from her infancy, childhood, young adulthood, and maturity, and celebrates elemental values about life that have provenance in the theology of West African Vodun. Her love story challenges her morally biased community to recant the "mass cruelty" (2) of its conditioned responses. She evinces Vodun and Judeo-Christian compassion when she says, "'Now, Pheoby, don't feel too mean wid de rest of 'em 'cause dey's parched up from not knowin' things'" (192). Janie Mae Crawford's quest to find a love that is unrestricted in extent and intensity has culminated in marriage to Vergible "Tea Cake" Woods, a scion of Vodun war god Ogoun, in appearance a "wild man of the woods," who is "quiet" and "dangerous" (Owusu 38). Damballah Ouedo, West African Vodun *loa*, or earth and watery underworld deity, resurfaces from *Jonah's Gourd Vine* to shape the trajectory of Janie Mae Crawford and Vergible "Tea Cake" Woods's dynamic whirlwind romance.

The protagonists in *Jonah's Gourd Vine*, Hurston's Vodun macho American novel, and *Their Eyes Were Watching God*, Hurston's Vodun feminist American novel, engage in individual quests for freedom to discover the spiritual meaning of their lives within the social context of their respective African-American Christian communities. Zora Neale Hurston represents their pilgrimages as provocative expressions of their twin Christian and Vodun souls. Their pilgrimages begin with outwardly seeking movements of escape from confinement inside the rather primitive Southern Baptist homes which fate has dealt them. Hurston's protagonists are motivated to discover existential selfhood by responding positively to desires identified with their deepest emotional urges. Hurston's novels of the African diaspora may be seen to revitalize the folksy traditional Christian communities into which their protagonists are born by setting into motion a quasi musical counterpoint in which the defining phrase may be traced to Hurston's perpetuating the theological rhythm and design of West African Vodun.

Hurston is arguably the first American novelist to make serious use of West African Vodun theology to depict African-American culture, which is ostensibly steeped in Southern Baptist Christianity. Hurston's fusion of Vodun and Christianity is so perfect as to have eluded notice by literati whose critical insights along with Ellease Sutherland's 1979 article have given rise to my exploratory investigation. Perceptively, Langston Hughes, in *The Big Sea* (1940), extols the innate artistic capacity Hurston demonstrates in writing her "tragic comic stories," which accommodate radically different, even polar opposite, modes of thinking and feeling: "She could make you laugh one minute and cry the next" (31). Henry Louis Gates, Jr., in his Afterword to *Their Eyes Were Watching God*, points out that Hurston is the first African-American novelist to combine "black vernacular speech and rituals" (354) with standard literary English narrative discourse and to succeed in reconciling these two strands to form a narrative "voice" that "shifts from third to a blend of first and third person (known as 'free indirect discourse')" (355). Hurston's cross-cultural fusion of linguistic and stylistic elements enriches *Their Eyes Were Watching God*, which Gates lauds as an innovative novel of "mythic realism . . . lush and dense within a lyrical black idiom" (357). Alice Walker praises Hurston's artistic accomplishment in exalting "a sense of black people as complete, complex, undiminished human beings, a sense that is lacking in so much black writing and literature" (85). Gwendolyn Mikell, in *African-American Pioneers in Anthropology*, stresses that Hurston "wished to emphasize the legitimacy and wholeness of black cultural institutions"; moreover, her anthropological investigations were motivated by her unwavering belief in "black cultural integrity" (66). Joseph E. Holloway, in *Africanisms in American Culture*, observes that in post-Civil War America "black churches" played a "strong role" in "helping blacks reorganize their culture after slavery ended" (x). While Hurston made "scathing indictments of the black middle class and black politics and of the eagerness with which blacks accepted desegregation and integration" (Mikell 66), her dogmatic ideology adamantly supported black Christian churches. Her sympathetic portrayals of Judeo Christianity testify to her recognition of the crucial role of religious pluralism in all-black African-American communities, where West African influences are even more pronounced. Although Hurston was born in Otasulga, Alabama, a racially integrated town, she identified so strongly with the ethnological values inherent in the concept of an all-black township that Eatonville, Florida, is widely touted as her legendary birthplace. It may be argued in literary and cultural terms that Hurston considered Eatonville to be her symbolic hometown because the concept of an all-black city is fertile ground on which she built the foundation for her artistic portrayals of African-American culture, which has roots deeply embedded in West African traditional religious beliefs.

Their Eyes Were Watching God refines Hurston's exploratory art of counterpoint in *Jonah's Gourd Vine* (1934). The 1934 novel contains scenes that opened it to lopsided and uninformed critical views and charges that the graphic accounts of Central African and West African rituals did not compare favorably with the preponderant Christian elements, claims that the anthropological material was not adequately integrated into the narrative. Failure to recognize, contextualize, and acknowledge the significance of Vodun dancing to African drum beats led to mixed book reviews. Josephine Pinckney's review attributed the overarching theological tenor of the novel to its Christian settings: the novel is "full of humor and folk notions; [it is] poetic, whether on the secular side or transposed into the biblical phraseology required by the many church scenes. Miss Hurston makes effective use of biblical rhythms in the passages that describe mass emotions quickening and becoming richer as they mount to a climax" (35). Andrew Burris's review misconstrued Hurston's aim as being to write "a novel about a backward Negro people" and to create "situations" for "them as mere pegs upon which to hang their dialect and their folkways," although, he admitted, the book is "a rich store of folklore" and Hurston captures "the lusciousness and beauty of the Negro dialect as have few others. John Buddy's sermon on the creation is the most poetic rendition of this familiar theme that we have yet encountered in print" (35-36). Burris concluded, "We can but hope that with time and further experience in the craft of writing, Zora Hurston will develop the ability to fuse her abundant material into a fine literary work" (36). These short-sighted reviewers nonetheless descry the novel's Vodun design; for them, Vodun elements in *Jonah's Gourd Vine* are local color and carry little intrinsic value. In relegating Vodun material to a subtextual level in *Their Eyes Were Watching God*, Hurston succeeds in imbuing the novel with West African Vodun as a pervasive natural force emanating from a cosmic doxology and harmonizing with the beliefs of Christianity.

The Christian theological perspective in *Their Eyes Were Watching God* coincides with the African traditional association of feminine spirituality with love. Similar in complexity to the Christian conversion of macho protagonist John Buddy after he slays a river guardian on his way to experiencing love and spiritual growth in *Jonah's Gourd Vine*, Janie Mae Crawford, feminist protagonist in *Their Eyes Were Watching God*, discovers an exhilarating but stormy path that paradoxically fills her heart with lofty insight into spiritual love. *Jonah's Gourd Vine* metamorphoses John Buddy's slaying of a river snake into an aesthetic trope that derives moral and religious significance from both Judeo-Christian symbology and West African Vodun cosmology, depicting the fall from grace of this young adult Christian man who slays a scion of Damballah Ouedo, the supreme Vodun divinity, and his torturous pilgrimage to release his troubled soul from hubris and pangs of guilt. Hurston slowly reveals to readers in his turbulent, agitated life a direct link between his salvific epiphany and the guardian river snake. In fulfillment of the promise of redemptive grace for John Buddy, whose patronymic extends to Pearson after he crosses Damballah Ouedo's river realm and does battle with a guardian snake, Hurston has Janie's understanding of life's ultimate truth crystallize at the moment she witnesses under a pear tree the consummation of male (bee) and female (flower) in "marriage" (13). The symbolism of the tree may also be read as the cross on which Christ suffered and died then ascended to reign at the right hand of God the Father. By means of her visionary art, Hurston evokes West African cosmology's fusion of the living and the sanctified spirits of the dead, the *loa*, through mystical unions made possible through the medium of nature divinities. Hurston's coupling of religions demonstrates that *Their Eyes Were Watching God* is a fulfillment of *Jonah's Gourd Vine* and suggests that Janie Mae Crawford's quest for truth in love and for personhood runs parallel to the messianic quest of the Vodun diaspora.

Their Eyes Were Watching God portrays Janie Mae Crawford as an ata-vistic incarnation of the West African Vodun goddess Ayida Ouedo, depict-ing the oscillating rise to respectability of this young woman who yearns to find her soul mate, a man with whom to escape "bourgeoisification" (Hurs-ton quoted in Mikell 51) and follow the trajectory of Vodun celestial goddess Ayida Ouedo so as to take delight in the love and happiness she anticipates wishfully when she reposes underneath a pear tree in bloom, a Genesaic tree of life, and contemplates the horizon. Janie's quest for love is commensurate with Ayida Ouedo's vast horizons. The film adaptation of Hurston's novel, also titled *Their Eyes Were Watching God*, shows the Vodun spiritual energy that Janie Mae Crawford exudes through her myriad acts of communion with nature. Panoramic camera shots portray her as a life force that gains suste-nance from the sky as a spiritual source. We see Janie gazing rapturously up into the blue sky in a devout state of bliss. The most striking instance of this poetically evoked association between Janie and the spiritual realm happens at the film's beginning. The camera pans out to a shot of Janie floating on her back in pond water and watching cirrus clouds floating in an azure sky. An expression of total contentment illuminates her face, which glows in reflec-tion of her spiritual ecstasy. This montage establishes her identification with Ayida Ouedo and contrasts sharply to her later victimization by Joe Starks when he uses violence to force her to emulate Erzulie Frieda. The film's romantic rendition of *Their Eyes Were Watching God* supplements, and of-fers an alternative approach to, the anthropological scientism Hurston fa-vored. African-American folklorist and anthropologist Lilith Dorsey retells the Dahomey Vodun Fon myth that accounts for the mercurial rise of Vodun theology: "Damballa and Aida Wedo are the Lwa [sic] responsible for bring-ing the religion of Vodun across the sea and sky from Africa to the Americas. Oftentimes, these divinities have been envisioned as snakes. In serpent form, Damballa and Ayida Ouedo left Africa with ancient knowledge of Vodun. Damballa took the route under the ocean, while Ayida Ouedo arched her serpent body across the sky to make the crown of the rainbow. They met on the island of Haiti, intertwining in an embrace of love that gave birth to the Vodou religion" (55). Significantly, traces of Hurston's searching for the more refined oblique narrative artistry of *Their Eyes Were Watching God* are evident in *Jonah's Gourd Vine*, a classic model of the Judeo-Christian Vodun American novel genre.

In *Jonah's Gourd Vine*, Hurston truncates anthropological material, which she incorporates in unobtrusive allusions that she carefully blends into her portrayal of character and American life. For example, mirrors may reflect both the living and, in *Jonah's Gourd Vine*, the consecrated spirits of the dead. Vodun believers may cover or remove mirrors in the home of a deceased man or woman so as to prevent a purgatorial image from reflecting in a mirror as occurs in Ian Softley's *The Skeleton Key* (2005), a movie about a Louisiana bayou gentleman paralyzed and muted by "dreams, spells, and curses," which are the staples of "blues lyrics" (Pastras 61). In *Jonah's Gourd Vine*, on her deathbed, Lucy Potts Pearson asserts her Christian belief while referring obliquely to the Vodun belief that a deceased person's image will appear in mirrors when she forbids Isie Pearson, her eldest daughter, to allow "de lookin' glass" to be covered (130). Later, John Buddy Pearson sees hallucinatory visions of Lucy Potts Pearson in the mirror of his mind: "Suddenly a seven-year-old picture came before him. Lucy's bright eyes in the sunken face. Helpless and defensive. The look. Above all, the look! John stared at it in fascinated horror for a moment. The sea of the soul, heaving after a calm, giving up its dead. He drove Hattie [Tyson] from his bed with vile imprecations" (145). After Lucy's premature death, John Buddy Pearson experiences spiritual rebirth. Lucy exerts a strong Christian influence that acts as a moral force. Hurston portrays Lucy as a conscience figure whose greatest wish is to bring her husband into closer alignment with traditional African-American values and codes of conduct. The vividness and genuineness of scenes in *Jonah's Gourd Vine* may be attributable, as scholars observe, to subtle resemblances between the fictional characters and the lives of Hurston's parents. Hurston fondly pays tribute to her father, Reverend John Hurston, and mother, Lucy Potts Hurston, in *Dust Tracks on a Road: An Autobiography* (1942).

The cosmic Vodun consciousness embraces a vast supernatural dualism that harnesses opposites, asserts mutual reciprocity between the realms of the living and the consecrated sprits of the dead, and attributes to supernatural deities—the *orishas* and the *loas*—the power of spiritual conviction to act as a driving force that affects the destiny of the living. West African Vodun envisions the universe as a multilateral unending interrelationship between the cool and lithesome elusiveness of feminine forces and the hot drive of masculine forces. The drum duet "Ibo" is native to Dahomey, a French West African colony from 1894 to 1960 before partition into Nigeria, Benin, and Togo. George Brandon explains that the "kings of Benin, Dahomey, and the Yoruba city-states all trace their origin back to Odua (Oduduwa), creator of the earth" (9). In this hierarchy, the "supreme being" is "Olodumare, the creator and sustainer of the universe, who nonetheless is remote from humans and has neither priesthood nor temples" (14). The "orisha" are "emanations directly from Olodumare": some "came from heaven," while "others were once human beings and died remarkable deaths" (14). "Ibo" appears in the form of musical notation in Hurston's painstakingly gathered "Songs of Worship" to major Vodun gods and illustrates this essential pattern in the alternating beats of sixteenth notes and rests played by the first drummer and the responsive mirroring pulses played by a second drummer (*Zora Neale Hurston: Folklore, Memoirs, and Other Writings* 554). In ways that complement her nonfiction writings and lend greater profundity to her research work as a cultural anthropologist, Hurston informs her earliest book-length fictional writings with the aesthetically fructifying principle of contradictory yet mutually interrelated forces at the heart of West African Vodun. Hurston's novels are particularly illuminating when each novel is read as an imaginative literary artifact amenable to critical exploration of the tandem coupling of West African Vodun spirituality with the traditional Christian religious beliefs and practices of African Americans in the Deep South. Paradoxically, this West African Vodun concept of oscillating complementarity and pluralistic perspective constitutes a unifying force that instills psychological complexity, poetic nuances, and spiritual intensity in Hurston's American novels.

Although Vodun originated in West Africa, this ancient religion reached the Americas by way of Haiti in the eighteenth century. Alfred Métraux avers, "A conglomeration of beliefs and rites of African origin, which, having been closely mixed with Catholic practice, [Haitian Voudoun] has come to be the religion of the greater part of the peasants and the urban proletariat of the black republic of Haiti" (15). Dorsey observes, "There is no official record of when the religion of [African Vodun] was introduced into North America, but most scholars agree it happened in New Orleans in the late 1700s" (58). Phil Pastras, a professor of English in southern California, observes in his scrupulously researched 2001 monograph on American jazz, "While a few scholars have denied that Roman Catholicism had any significant influence on [Vodun], by far the majority view [Voudoun] as a syncretic religion, developed in Haiti, that fused West African religions with Catholicism, along with perhaps some Native American forms and imagery. A similar fusion appeared wherever African slaves came in contact with Catholicism—*Santería* in Cuba and *Candomblé* in Brazil are widely regarded by scholars as parallel phenomena, parallel to each other and to [Haitian Voudoun]" (61).

During extensive travels in the American South and the Caribbean archipelago, Hurston wrote more than a million words in documenting her investigations of Negro folklore, religious practices, and spiritual beliefs. These meticulously prepared materials were subsequently made more readily available in the Library of America volume entitled *Zora Neale Hurston: Folklore, Memoirs, and Other Writings* (1995). Hurston's fieldwork memoirs help to lay the groundwork for analytical interpretation of Janie Mae Crawford's mythic West African Vodun love quest in *Their Eyes Were Watching God*. Examination of Hurston's ambitious attempt to incorporate the symbology of Vodun cosmology in *Jonah's Gourd Vine* reinforces elucidation of *Their Eyes Were Watching God* as an outgrowth of Hurston's anthropological investigations. Textual analysis suggests that Hurston has reinvented the American novel as a result of her systematic yet thoroughly artistic representation of morally inflected West African Vodun theological principles. The benchmark novels she wrote are much more than merely fictionalized accounts of the lives of African-American denizens. Their ideological foundation in Vodun theology confers mythic overtones upon John Buddy Pearson and Janie Mae Crawford as fictional characters that illuminate the liberated imagination of Hurston and shed new light on the all-black incorporated municipality of Eatonville, located six miles north of Orlando, Florida, which Alice Walker visited in 1975, because, Walker writes in "Looking for Zora," it was "Zora Neale Hurston's birthplace" (395).

Hurston went to New Orleans to study Hoodoo, which is the local Louisiana variant of Haitian Voudoun, after she graduated with a bachelor of arts degree at Barnard College and sojourned in Florida and Alabama. Her research on New Orleans Hoodoo occupied her daily routine from August 1928 to April 1929 and from October to December 1929. She began to write *Jonah's Gourd Vine* in August 1933, and she finished writing it on October 3, 1933. While working on her Ph.D. in anthropology at Columbia University in 1935, she accepted a Guggenheim Foundation fellowship and went to Haiti, where her field work provided evidence of theologically significant cultural similarities among black communities in the American South, the West Indies, and Haiti, which share a common Fon, Ibo, and Yoruba heritage traceable to West African Vodun. Her anthropological studies during the 1930s were initially distributed in short press run publications of *Mules and Men* (1935), *Tell My Horse* (1938), and *Dust Tracks on a Road* and have served as a path-finding footprint for researchers to follow. Her anthropological research, which she pursued for nearly a decade, empowered her with a high level of intellectual understanding and cultural awareness that jelled and skyrocketed to an artistic zenith when she wrote her critically acclaimed second novel, *Their Eyes Were Watching God*. During the period between September 22, 1936, and December 19, 1936, Hurston completed *Their Eyes Were Watching God*. Hurston discerns, in *Tell My Horse*, that West African Vodun is "a religion of creation and life. It is the worship of the sun, the water and other natural forces, but the symbolism is no better understood than that of other religions and consequently is taken too literally" (376). As a gifted novelist, Hurston explores the hidden dimensions of meaning in West African Vodun theology by embedding in her artful representations of mundane reality theologically resonant layers of meaning residing beneath the surface of monotheist Vodun hierarchic cosmology.

The interdisciplinary concept of syncretism is central to understanding Hurston's aesthetic approach to the theological novel genre. In historical and contemporary terms, West African and Central African Vodun theology comprises a belief system linked to myriad indigenous native cults and sects.

Vodun coexists, in the Americas, with Catholicism and the predominant Judeo Christian Protestant religious denominations and, in the Caribbean archipelago, with Roman Catholicism, which gained legions of converts, starting in the fifteenth century, during successive colonization by the empires of Portugal, France, and England. When we excavate Hurston's novel *Their Eyes Were Watching God*, foundational West African Vodun rises to the surface enhancing the visible layer of Christianity. No mere embellishment, symbolic imagery richly reveals interpenetrating concepts drawn from Christian-American cultural tradition and African-American beliefs and practices. Symbolical language and dramatic scenes of confrontation and conflict conceal points of convergence between Judeo Christianity and Vodun. This linguistic and aesthetic shield protects, yet ultimately evokes, *Their Eyes Were Watching God*'s theological roots in ancient West African Vodun cosmology.

Hurston's mentor at Columbia University, Melville J. Herskovits (1895-1963), demonstrates in his pioneering October 1937 study *The American Negro: A Study in Racial Crossing* that African Americans emanate from "three principal racial stocks of the world: Negro ancestry from Africa, Caucasian from northern and western Europe, and Mongoloid (American Indian) from southeastern America and the Caribbean Islands" (4). He argues convincingly that the American Negro is not a "new race," but constitutes "a homogeneous population group" (82). The vast majority of Negro Americans were descendants of slaves exported from "the Guinea coast of West Africa" (xiii). Since "the offspring of a slave was also a slave," "mixed-bloods" are Negroes (3). In *Cultural Dynamics* (1964), Herskovits argues for the permanence and enduring strength of West African culture: "West African cultures and their New World derivatives afford an instance of retention of an original focus under forced acculturation" (188-89). He asserts, "These West African societies are among the largest in the non-literate world. Their technological equipment is advanced, their economies complex, their political systems sophisticated and their social structures well organized and administered. Their folklore is noted for its subtlety . . . The focus of these cultures is on religion in all its manifestations—belief-systems, worldview, and ritual" (189). Herskovits emphasizes that West African Vodun theology accommodates Christianity, not the reverse, "In West Africa, tribal gods had been freely borrowed, and there was no reason why the Christian concept of the universe and the powers that rule it, which the Negroes encountered, could not equally well be incorporated into their system of belief" (189). Herskovits stresses the symbiotic relationship between Vodun theology and Christianity, observing, "Syncretism is most strikingly exemplified" in the way "New World Negroes in Catholic countries of the New World" identify "African deities with the saints of the Church" (190). Herskovits avers that Haitian villagers identify "Legba, the trickster of the West African Dahomeans and Yorubans," with Saint Anthony, "the patron of the poor"; Haitians respect Legba as "an old man who wanders about, clad in tatters," and Damballa invites admiration as "the Dahomean rainbow-serpent" often identified with Saint Patrick (190).

Hurston's novels use elemental nature imagery—water, air, fire, and earth—to portray ways in which West African Vodun is deeply embedded in the collective unconscious, hence in the folklore and culture, of African Americans, even those who have been taught to worship God under the auspices of Southern Baptist religious beliefs. Both *Jonah's Gourd Vine* and *Their Eyes Were Watching God* conflate the Christian sacrament of baptism by immersion in water, as when John the Baptist baptized Jesus by total immersion in the waters of the Jordan River in Asia, with the Vodun worship of Esu-Elegba as "the opener of gates" leading to "opportunities" (Hurston, *Tell My Horse* 382). Hurston reserves the epithet "Papa" for the opener of the gate to the spiritual life: "Legba Attibon is the god of the gate. He rules the gate of the hounfort [a sequestered site for observance of Vodun rituals], the entrance to the cemetery and he is also Baron Carrefour, Lord of the cross-roads. The way to all things is in his hands . . . The picture of John the Baptist is used to represent Papa Legba" (*Tell My Horse* 393). Hurston uses narrative counterpoint to evoke a continuum at the Vodun crossroad of art and life. Key episodes in *Jonah's Gourd Vine* and *Their Eyes Were Watching God* show that Hurston, by dint of her intellectual imagination and ability to evoke theological resonances, merges the resilience of Southern Baptist religious observance with West African Vodun spiritual consciousness.

The title *Jonah's Gourd Vine* is symbolic of the way John Buddy Pearson's married life with Lucy Potts Pearson coincides with Jonah being swallowed by a cow whale in Holy Scripture. Just as God provided a whale to prevent Jonah from drowning in the sea, so, too, John Buddy Pearson seeks refuge from the vicissitudes of his turbulent demigod-like life and in the time-honored institutions of the family and marriage. But the holy sacrament of marriage and his life with Lucy Potts are undermined by his attack against the Vodun guardian of river god Damballah Ouedo. *Jonah's Gourd Vine* shows that the values of Judeo Christianity and Vodun need to be respected in order for John Buddy Pearson to attain peace of mind. Together, Lucy Potts Pearson, a devout Christian, along with a triumvirate of Vodun earth and water deities succeed in transforming his hubris, or excessive pride, into feelings of guilt and contrition for his slaying of a guardian river snake, for his misogynist treatment of Lucy, and for his extramarital amours-fous (mad loves).

In the stunningly impressive opening chapter of *Jonah's Gourd Vine*, heroic protagonist John Buddy daringly swims through the snake-filled waters of a tributary of the Alabama River, reaches the other side, and symbolically sloughs off his futureless life as an ignorant, poverty-stricken Negro who was born out-of-wedlock to a house slave. Instead of binding John over to Captain Mimms, a prosperous plantation overseer whose cash profits are stained with the blood of slaves he whipped to death, Amy Crittenden has told her son to go and work for Judge Alf Pearson. Her override demotes Ned, who is not John's natural father, to the role of "Mah-lah-sah, the guardian of the doorsill" (Hurston, *Tell My Horse* 382). Ned Crittenden, John's stepfather, bellows "'Shet dat door, John" (2). Ned foreshadows John Buddy's abuse of Damballah's river guardian when he batters Amy with a "raw hide whip" (8). Amy denounces Ned's unchristian actions "'He didn't got no business hittin' me wid dat raw hide and neither chokin' me neither. Jesus, Jesus, Jesus, Jeesus!'" (8-9). Her Christian belief is buttressed by her keen eye for nature's hidden secrets.

Amy, whose name means "love," emulates Mami Wata, an ancient Vodun water deity, "a joyous goddess who represents the sea" and "a mermaid" (Dorsey 24). Amy warns John, conflating her awe of the river god Damballah Ouedo and guardian snake with her dread of the raw-hide whip: "'G'wan, son, and be keerful uh dat foot-log 'cross de creek. De Songahatchee is strong water, and look out under foot so's yuh don't git snake bit.'" (11). He celebrates his leave-taking with a Vodun prayer: "John plunged on down to the Creek, singing a new song and stomping the beats. The Big Creek thundered among its rocks and whirled on down. So John sat on the foot-log and made some words to go with the drums of the Creek" (12). John sits on a log at the edge of the woods all night before his baptismal swim across the Big Creek confirms him as a hero whose family love and physical stamina mark his passage from adolescence to manhood. The key to his character is in the vision he has in total darkness before "the moon came up" of laughing "people" who "had lots of daughters" (12). This sexual fantasy is inspired by Erzulie Frieda, a sex symbol who remains childless yet is a "female counterpart of Damballah" (Hurston, *Tell My Horse* 383). I interpret Hurston's pairing Damballah Ouedo with Erzulie Frieda as a "counterpart" to reflect the difference between watery abodes that accommodate life, such as oceans (coral reefs), lakes, rivers, and streams, and lush waterfalls whose precipitous downward rush and rapid flow are beautiful but give no safe harbor for regeneration of life forms. Sexual desires shape John Buddy Pearson's conduct as a married man and career as a Christian minister. The rising of the sun fills him with sexual energy: "No telling how many girls might be living on the new and shiny side of the Big Creek. John almost trumpeted exultantly at the new sun. He breathed lustily" (12). His Vodun prayer is answered when he arrives at the mansion, where Alf Pearson hires him to work on the cotton plantation. His prayer to his Christian "Lawd" for "mercy" (25) is answered when he memorizes the "alphabet" (26) and learns to read at the community schoolhouse, where the schoolmaster, Lucy Potts's uncle, changes his name to John Pearson, legitimizing him. Unwittingly, he crisscrosses Judeo-Christian and African Vodun cultural boundaries. His Christmas gifts to Lucy's family juxtapose Christian adoration and Vodun exoticism; for example, he puts "a huge China doll on the tree for Lucy" (65). In Asian Vodun lore, Ayida Ouedo's retinue consists of almond-eyed dancers whose skin resembles polished sandalwood.

Lucy Potts weds John Buddy Pearson despite her parents' disapproval. Her nuptial bliss is marred by ambivalent feelings: "The aisle seemed long, long! But it was like climbing up the stairs to glory. Her trembling fear she left on the climb. When she rode off beside John at last she said, 'John Buddy, look lak de moon is givin' sunshine'" (79). Newlywed bride Lucy Potts Pearson is an incarnation of the moon, whose piercing light reflects changing phases in the interrelationship of Earth and the sun.

Viewed through the lens of Vodun cosmology, Lucy Potts Pearson is a feminine incarnation of the moon, which reflects sunlight refracted by Earth's shadow. John Buddy Pearson is a masculine incarnation of the sun, which, like a virile man, has the energy to generate life. In the hierarchy of Vodun drums, the drum representing the moon takes precedence over the drum representing the sun. Although Lucy intends to express how proud she is to be married to John, her likening of the moon to the sun evokes the theme of appearance and reality and is symbolic in an ambivalent way of thinking that is typical of Vodun. Since her Pottstown family is much more prosperous than his backwoods step-family, their wedding is upstaged by his primogeniture in a union resulting from a white master's dominance over a female house slave. Vodun ritual evokes this rift between Lucy as an emblem of white patriarchy and John as a morally charged symbol of righteous retribution. This reversal, in which Vodun interrogates a socioeconomic divide caused by racial discrimination, suggests a hex on John, who mirrors societal angst perpetrated by slavery. Lucy is aware of her societal dominance when she meets and marries a man who is unable to provide for her in the manner to which she has grown accustomed. Vodun natural law imbues Lucy's romantic allusion to the full moon with ominous portentousness. Dorsey's description of the divine twins of the Haitian Vodoun pantheon coincides with Hurston's depiction of John Buddy Pearson and Vergible "Tea Cake" Woods as solar men and Lucy Potts Pearson and Janie Mae Crawford as lunar ladies: "The Marassa are the sacred twins of the Haitian Vodou. Named Mawu and Lisa, they are the Moon and the Sun, a divine symmetry of the female and male energies of the cosmos. . . According to legend at first these two were separate, living on opposite sides of the sky, until one day there was an eclipse. They literally and figuratively came together and created seven pairs of twins" (Dorsey 55). Both John Buddy Pearson and Janie Mae Crawford have a two-sided or "twin" personality, comprised of a primary personhood and a secondary black soulfulness that springs into being when precipitated by an antithetical soul mate. The liberation of the repressed conscience of John and the liberation of the suppressed ego of Janie, who sublimates her desire to express love by accepting the world in a cosmic, all-embracing spirituality, form underlying plots that unfold, creating tension and suspense.

Vodun earth and water creation divinity Damballah Ouedo is the binding force that brings love into the lives of Hurston's solar macho male and lunar lady female protagonists. John Buddy and Lucy Potts live on opposite sides of the Alabama River, separated by economic and social barriers. In the schoolroom, John lags behind, while Lucy stands at the top of her class. The marriage of Janie Mae Crawford and Vergible "Tea Cake" Woods is comparable because they, too, belong to different social classes. As a feminine emblem of a prelapsarian Vodun obedient Eve, Janie plays the roles chosen for her by Nanny, Logan Killicks, Joe Starks, and Vergible "Tea Cake" Woods. Logan Killicks puts the millstone of plowing the earth around her neck. Joe Starks keeps her nose to the grindstone and displays her as a flashy showpiece to polish his political image. Vergible "Tea Cake" Woods breezes into town, then he sweeps her off her feet, and finally, he takes her over the rainbow.

The steady and confident forward movement of her expansive arc of life parallels the devout and stolid character of Lucy. When she is at her wit's end, Janie passes womanly judgment on Killicks and Starks. Similarly, Lucy speaks in oblique judgment of John: "De hidden wedge will come tuh light someday, John. Mark mah words" (129). John Buddy Pearson engages in a clandestine secret life that deviates from the norms of the Judeo-Christian doctrine he preaches. In contrast, Janie Crawford is scrupulous in the way she confides to Logan Killicks, her first husband, her wish to leave him, in the way she loyally endures twenty years of a loveless marriage to Joe Starks, and in the way she is true to Vergible Woods as the love of her life. Hurston depicts the conflicts between Lucy and John in *Jonah's Gourd Vine* and between Janie and her social world in *Their Eyes Were Watching God* as outcomes of social and economic differences in their backgrounds to show how their marriages parallel the bonding of the sun and the moon and are comprehensible with reference to Vodun cosmological theology.

In traditional folkloric African Vodun and Haitian Voudoun symbology, Damballah is "the great source," because the other Vodun divinities "must come to Damballah to get the permission and the power" to "grant" the prayers of their devotees (*Tell My Horse* 381). John Buddy makes a huge mistake when he defies Damballah Ouedo. Although his love attraction to thirteen-year-old Lucy Potts culminates in a formal wedding at the Macedonia Baptist Church, their marriage is marked by West African Vodun as a result of his overzealousness in wrangling with the guardian river snake. His encounter with Big Creek's thunder and whirl invoking the authority of Damballah Ouedo resurfaces in his courtship of Lucy, which takes place under the auspices of a veiled ceremonial Vodun worship. During these religious observances, the liturgical cadences of West African drumbeats are analogous to the sounding of church bells. They are also associated with Shango, the Vodun deity of thunder and lightning and the lord of the drum and fire, images that coincide with the wrath of the Judeo-Christian God in Holy Scripture. Devotees of Shango, the owner of the Bata, three double-headed drums, consider him the ruler of music and the art of dance. The drumbeats onomatopoeically imitate Shango's thunder. The rhythmical invocation to the African-American dancers, sounded by "dance drums of Africa," which are fashioned from kid-skin, is as prayerful as a Christian minister's 'Let us pray' call to worship. Kata-Kumba, the great drum, displays the divine handiwork of "priests and sits in majesty in the juju house" and honors the born-again heartbeat of a new day, for Kata-Kumba is "the drum with the man skin that is dressed with human blood, which is beaten with a human shin-bone and speaks to gods as a man and to men as a God. Then they beat upon the drum and dance" (*Jonah's Gourd Vine* 29). Hurston's omniscient narrator notes, "Hollow hand clapping for the bass notes. Heel and toe stomping for the little one. Ibo tune corrupted with Nango. Congo gods talking in Alabama" (30). The atmosphere of African Vodun superimposes hot cosmological images on the reality of the Alabama croplands: "Too hot for words. Fiery drum clapping. / 'Less [Let us] burn dat old moon down to a nub!" (31). Presently the "fire died. The moon died. The shores of Africa receded. They went to sleep" (31).

These vibrant scenes anticipate the fiery passions of John Buddy Pearson and the birth of his children, but also foreshadow the decline and death of Lucy Potts Pearson. Her life wanes, from the full moon shining on her wedding night, to the gibbous moons of her pregnancies, and finally, to the crescent moon of the somber wake at her deathbed. Vodun imagery suggests that her power ("the furious music of the little drum whose body was still in Africa, but whose soul sung around a fire in Alabama") adds impetus to her Christian faith after her untimely and premature death (30). Her death ignites a sporadic awakening of his conscience that climaxes when he falls into a dream trance at the wheel of his automobile. The locomotive that kills him is a symbol of his serpentine rise to awareness of his ancestral Vodun Judeo-Christian guilt. Like Jonah, he disobeys God; moreover, he, like Adam, succumbs to the temptation of flaunting his macho attraction, incited by the allure of archetypal Eve figures. Vodun imagery suggests the power of Lucy Potts Pearson, an atavistic archetype symbol of Mother Africa, is greatest right after she has accepted John Buddy's ardent marriage proposal.

In terms of Vodun's rich symbology, John Buddy Pearson is an incarnation of the sun, which has the power to generate life. *Jonah's Gourd Vine's* plot shows that his transgression against Damballah Ouedo puts him into tight lifelong relationship with the slain river guard. His psychic link to

Vodun puts him under an obligation to atone for his sin. Ancient pagan law sanctioned the sacrifice of a young woman to appease the spirit-gods. His sense of double-edged guilt goads him to exact retribution by "beating" Lucy Potts Pearson "severely" until he "felt better" (145). His embittered expressions of frustration do not atone for his desecration of a Vodun nature divinity in the symbolic Songanatchee river of life; indeed, his repressed guilt precipitates his violation of Lucy's Christian sensibility. Nevertheless, Lucy's girlish naiveté awakens his conscience, illuminating God as omniscient creator of all humankind. After Lucy confronts John about his extramarital affairs, his Vodun preaching conflates Vodun and Christianity: "'You are de same God, Ah / Dat heard de sinner man cry. / Same God dat sent de zigzag lightning tuh / Join de mutterin' thunder. / Same God dat holds de elements / In uh unbroken chain of controllment. / Same God dat hung on Calvary and died. / Dat we might have a right tuh de tree of life'" (88). His willful conflation of Christianity and Vodun is defiant and worshipful: "Some new . . . praise-giving name for God, every time he knelt in church. He rolled his African drum up to the altar, and called his Congo Gods by Christian names. One night at the altar-call he cried out his barbaric poetry to his 'Wonder-workin' God so effectively that three converts came through religion under the sound of his voice" (89). At the funeral, the preacher delivers "a barbaric requiem poem" (201), in which John Buddy is a brute known only to "God": "'Oh Death who gives a cloak to the man who walked naked in the world. And the hearers wailed with a feeling of terrible loss. They beat upon the O-go-doe, the ancient drum. . . Their hearts turned to fire and their shinbones leaped unknowing to the drum. Not Kata-Kumba, the drum of triumph, that speaks of great ancestors and glorious wars. Not the little drum of kid-skin, for that is to dance with joy and to call to mind birth and creation, but O-go-doe, the voice of Death. . . He wuz uh man, and nobody knowed 'im but God'" (202).

At the beginning of the long second chapter, train imagery invokes the sheer power of Damballah Ouedo, working through Ogoun, Vodun god of iron and war, when John Buddy Pearson is suddenly "conscious of a great rumbling" as "the train schickalacked up to the station and stopped" (15). In the eyes of community observers, he cuts a somewhat comic figure as he stares at "the panting monster," while "that great eye beneath the cloud-breathing smoke-stack glared and threatened," and "the engine's fiery sides seemed to expand and contract like a fiery-lunged monster" (16). His mute fright prompts the train engineer to blow "a sharp blast on the whistle," causing him to "start violently," which makes "the crowd roar" (16). The townsmen's laughter ("'You ain't never seed nothin' dangerous lookin' lak dat befo', is yuh?'") changes to respect when John retorts "'But hits uh pretty thing, too'" (16). At the end of the second chapter, John shows heroic bravery in the face of Lucy's fear. In nature, a river snake inspires fear but unleashes violent action only at the behest of human will. Lucy Potts confides to John Buddy, "'Everytime Ah go 'cross dat foot-log Ah think maybe Ah might fall in and den he'll bite me'" (34). She warns John, "'When he see somebody comin' he go in his hole, all ready for yuh and lay dere and dare yuh tuh bother 'im'" (34). The novel links the train as panting monster to this defensive river sovereign that takes action as a subordinate to creation god Damballah Ouedo whose domain is earth and water, including rivers and oceans.

At the end, John falls asleep at the wheel of his automobile, and his sudden death when a train runs into his automobile mirrors his earlier fight with the river snake, when, we recall, "He stepped cautiously into the water. The snake went on guard, slowly, insolently. Lucy was terrified. Suddenly, he snatched the foot-log from its place and, leaning far back to give it purchase, he rammed it home upon the big snake and held it there. The snake bit at the log again and again in its agony, but finally the biting and the thrashing ceased. John fished the snake out and stretched it upon the grass" (34). Vodun theological cosmology links his death at a railway crossing to Vodun spirit-god Damballah and to Ogoun, the Vodun "god of iron" (Owusu 38), hence of industry and technology, including railroads. The train is a double metaphor that evokes the river moccasin, guardian of Damballah Ouedo, whose presence is symbolically associated with the river. In *Jonah's Gourd Vine*, Hurston's use of poetical nature imagery to portray motivational traits and latent qualities of character traceable to African-American cultural roots in Vodun theological cosmology complements the folkloristic cultural beliefs and practices she encountered among devout Haitians practicing their religion. In traditional American lore, the horse power of the locomotive earned it the appellation of iron horse in 1840. The locomotive that strikes John reprises John's war-like attack on Damballah Ouedo's guardian river snake and invokes the ancillary power of Ogoun, the Vodun god of war associated with iron weaponry. In Haiti, folklorist and anthropologist Hurston saw that altars devoted to worship of Damballah had an "iron representation of the snake" (*Tell My Horse* 381).

In Vodun doctrine, crossings and crossroads are sites where the spirit separates from the body of a devotee or the spirit of an ancestor or of a relative fills a devotee with powerful emotions. In both the water crossing and the railroad crossing, death parts the material from the metaphysical. Significantly, John Buddy Pearson is "looking inward" when his own spirit is parted from his flesh. His contemplation of Lucy's reincarnation in the form of Sister Sally Lovelace of Pilgrim Rest Baptist Church is a veiled allusion to spiritual rebirth, a tenet of both Vodun theology and Christianity. The belief that an individual comes back in another form has West African provenance. John Buddy, who killed Damballah's fearsome defender, ultimately suffers the same fate that he dealt:

> He had prayed for Lucy's return and God had answered with Sally [Lovelace].
> He drove on but half-seeing the railroad from looking inward. The engine
> struck the car squarely and hurled it about like a toy. John was thrown out and
> lay perfectly still. Only his foot twitched a little (200).

Vodun deities Damballah Ouedo, Ogoun, and Esu-Elegbara reclaim and redeem John Buddy. Ogoun, an iron-fisted war god, makes the railroad intersection a war zone where the iron horse scores a direct hit and mangles John
Buddy's car. Vodun's superlative *loa* Damballah Ouedo puts John Buddy
Pearson into a lulling trance-like peace of mind, which allows him to understand his memories of Lucy Potts and Sally Lovelace, ironically at the moment he loses his hold on life. Papa Legba opens a gate to permit his passage
from physical body into the spiritual domain as a metaphysical soul.

Hurston's depiction of John Buddy Pearson's death galvanizes a triumvirate of Vodun *loas* coming alive and infusing the macho protagonist's suffering a violent death with theological overtones. Even though John Buddy
Pearson found happiness in his marriage to Sally Lovelace, which constitutes
a genuine Christian love story, *Jonah's Gourd Vine* superposes ancient
African Vodun theological values to retell the archetypal tale of the fall of
mankind from innocence and redemption through faith in the power of
prayer. Hurston portrays two women at the heart of two love stories in
Jonah's Gourd Vine: Lucy's relationship with John Buddy Pearson is in-
spired by the moral allegory of Adam and Eve's temptation in the garden of
Eden. Hurston extends the Judeo-Christian theme of obedience to God in the
Book of Genesis to the Vodun theme of retribution in *Jonah's Gourd Vine*.
Yet, John Buddy Pearson dies a happy man because he feels gratitude that his
prayer for the return of Lucy Potts Pearson was answered when God sent
Sally Lovelace and she agreed to be his wife. Lucy is the light of his life, an
archetypal Eve, spiritually reborn when he wedded Sally Lovelace, an arche-
typal feminist variant of the resurrected Christ in the New Testament.

Comparably to *Jonah's Gourd Vine*, *Their Eyes Were Watching God* has
an interlocking pattern that interweaves the soulful resilience of Negro culture and traditional West African belief. After "Joseph Starks" (93), Janie's
second husband, has died, at his funeral the Elks band plays the church hymn
"Safe in the Arms of Jesus" to the beat of "a dominant [African] drum
rhythm" so that the townspeople "stepped off smartly" as they "filed inside"
to pay homage to the man whom they regard as a Christian Saint Joseph
figure and as a scion of Papa Legba, spiritual leader and patron god. But, as
archetypal gatekeeper guarding the juncture of "rags" (12) and riches, Mayor
Starks has emulated Legba Attibon: "The Little Emperor of the cross-roads
was leaving Orange County as he had come—with the out-stretched hand of
power" (88). The narrative counterpoints the Negro spiritual in two ways.
Spiritually, it evokes Papa Legba as the Vodun deity solemnly standing at the

crossroad of life and death. Cross-culturally, it identifies Mayor Starks as the messianic gate opener who took his constituents from the poverty and martyrdom of Jesus Christ to the prosperity of Eatonville. As with many of the Vodun-Christian juxtapositions in *Their Eyes Were Watching God*, pairing of Vodun and Christianity reprises, fleshes out, and reinforces a pattern begun in Hurston's maiden novel. *Jonah's Gourd Vine* reveals cultural African-American hybridity in John Buddy Pearson, an attribute demonstrated in his initiation into manhood, his relationship with Lucy, and his passionate priestly Vodun-Christian preaching.

   Jonah's Gourd Vine is a paragon of amalgamation and intricate complexity. Hurston commingles Judeo-Christian symbology and Vodun nature imagery in her depiction of John Buddy Pearson as he achieves his rites of passage through the maze of life. *Jonah's Gourd Vine* is a double-edged Bildungsroman that traces his upward socioeconomic mobility as husband, father, and churchman, and, simultaneously, his Orphic descent into the lovesick depths of his Vodun American soul. John Buddy is a new African-American scion of the biblical Adam, and Lucy Potts, who urges him to hunt down and kill the snake, is his Eve. Rather than showing respect by allowing a creature of nature to return peacefully to its abode in the depths of the river, he slew the guardian of Damballah's river of life. This transgression tinctures, and blights, the rest of his days. At the end of the novel's long second chapter, John responds heroically when a "'cotton-mouf moccasin'" snake terrifies Lucy, who reacts as a Christian and tells him, "'Ooh, John, Ahm so glad you kilt dat ole devil'" (33-34). Hurston depicts his slaying of the water mocassin graphically as a Herculean task accomplished by a cow-towed hero who wants to impress the smart, rich "girl," with her "blue sunbonnet" precariously "lying back of her neck," with his physical courage and perseverance (33). In her last and only all-white community novel, *Seraph on the Suwanee* (1948), Zora Neale Hurston parodies her portrayal in *Jonah's Gourd Vine* of archetypal woman (Eve) successfully tempting archetypal man (Adam) to partake of a delicious, but forbidden apple, in disobedience to God the Father. Jim Meserve takes firm hold of a snake but when it almost injures him, he is so mortified, humbled, and humiliated that he tells Arvay, his wife, that he will not come home again until she lures him back to her. This homespun scene neutralizes the potency of the theological meanings her earlier three novels—*Jonah's Gourd Vine*, *Their Eyes Were Watching God*, and *Moses, Man of the Mountain*—attribute to snakes, serpents, and reptiles. Vodun devotees may detect in the ostensibly heroic deed of John Buddy undertones of sacrilege and violation, while Christian readers may chortle over the humorous image fraught with Freudian undertones that evokes his manful struggle to overcome his baser instincts and evince the moral restraint of his Judeo-Christian upbringing. This key moment in *Jonah's Gourd Vine* is an arabesque that prefigures, indeed predetermines, the novel's rising action and tragic dénouement. If Hurston had omitted the revisionist Vodun retelling of the temptation of Adam and Eve in Genesis, the novel would still figure as a highly sophisticated exemplary African-American contribution to the Bildungsroman genre but with a twist.

John Buddy Pearson is afflicted by Eshu, an unpredictable tricksy aspect of Papa Legba. A sacred Yoruban fable illustrates that Eshu is a Vodun spirit of discord that detests harmony. When Eshu observes two farmers walking side-by-side being in total agreement about everything, he finds this bland sweetness repugnant. He walks in-between the men. He asks the men what color his hat is. The man to his right says "black," but the man on his left says "white." The two men argue, not realizing that Eshu's hat is black on one side, white on the other side, and Eshu is pleased with the discord (Dorsey 26-27). The soul of John Buddy Pearson is afflicted because the "ego-soul" or "ti-bon-anj"(small good angel), which belongs to the Christian preacher side of his personality, is in conflict with the "gros-bon-anj" (big good angel), which is "an immortal and divine spirit that manifests itself in human life" (Desmangles 67). No matter how well-intentioned when viewed as a recuperative act that counterpoints Adam and Eve's disobedience in acquiescing to a smooth-talking serpent, the act of slaying a river snake runs counter to Vodun worship of Damballah Ouedo. Furthermore, in Holy Scripture, God denounces but does not kill the serpent for tempting Adam and Eve. God changes the serpent into a snake, an adaptation that responds to Adam and Eve's moral decision to disobey God in order to emulate God through pursuit of wisdom and knowledge. In *Jonah's Gourd Vine*, the snake symbolizes moral courage to preserve and protect the river of life from desecration by transgressors against Damballah Ouedo.

From the very beginning of courtship, John Buddy Pearson strains against the strictures of traditional Christian religious mores and practices. He is heedless of the moral rightness or wrongness of his actions because his unacknowledged guilt makes him ride roughshod over Lucy Potts for her loyalty to Christian moral values. His victorious entanglement with Damballah Ouedo's river snake guardian bolsters his ego with false pride that blinds him to his sinful mercenary attitude. Jonah does not listen when God asks him to tell Ninevah to mend their wicked ways. Similarly, John does not listen to his Vodun conscience. Hurston's admiration for earth and water divinity Damballah opens this new dimension in the novel. Hurston views Damballah as "the highest and most powerful of all the gods" (*Tell My Horse* 381). John's destruction of the river snake marks him as a tragic hero whose love for Lucy is doomed to be overshadowed by her husband's act of aggression against Damballah Ouedo's river guardian. He does not lovingly rescue Lucy from the vicissitudes of life's harsher realities; instead, he wages a battle against the life-giving and life-sustaining power of Vodun nature deity Damballah. The novel sets the hubris of John, a misguided Christian man whose unmindful rescue of Lucy transforms him into an archetypal pagan hero, against both Damballah Ouedo's grandeur and Jesus Christ's humility. Unwittingly, he traverses both Christian and Vodun religious boundaries. As a folklore specialist, Hurston highlights a remarkable conflation of Vodun theological imagery with Hebraic Old Testament and Christian New Testament symbology when she observes that Damballah's "signature is the ascending snakes on a rod or a crucifix" (*Tell My Horse* 382). Hurston's portrayals of John Buddy Pearson and Janie Mae Crawford emulate theological syncretism. Hurston observes, "Damballah Ouedo is the supreme Mystère and his signature is the serpent. All over Haiti it is well established that Damballah is identified as Moses. The rod of Moses is said to have been a subtle serpent. All over the Southern United States, the British West Indies and Haiti there are reverent tales of Moses and his magic. It is hardly possible that all of them sprang up spontaneously in these widely separated areas on the blacks coming in contact with Christianity after coming to the Americas. It is more probable that there is a tradition of Moses as the great father of magic scattered over Africa and Asia" (*Tell My Horse* 378).

The title of *Jonah's Gourd Vine* alludes directly to the Book of Jonah, but this biblical image of the wilting vine may also be interpreted as a symbolic allusion to the Vodun divinity Damballah. There is an implicit link between John Buddy Pearson and Vodun river imagery in *Jonah's Gourd Vine*. This link coincides with Hurston's observation of the association in Haitian Voudoun theology of Moses with the symbol of the serpent. In the Old Testament Book of Exodus, the staff of Moses symbolizes his role as a patriarch (shepherd), leading the Israelites (flock) out of bondage. In Vodun ritual worship, the houngan (Vodun priest or shaman) uses a gourd-shaped rattle to call on the *loa*. Similarly, the title of *Their Eyes Were Watching God* refers to the Christian God, yet directs attention skyward, to the transatlantic "horizon" bridging Africa and America (1).

Hurston incorporates a salient personification of drums as "Congo gods talking in Alabama" (30) in *Jonah's Gourd Vine* into an all-pervasive element that permeates the structural design of *Their Eyes Were Watching God*. Subtly, Hurston stratifies her Vodun novel into an allegorical pattern that evokes periods in the development of West African civilization. Metaphorically, Janie Mae Crawford's marriages to three men representing different social and cultural milieus metaphorically evoke stages in West Africa's history, beginning with the inception of Vodun theology and the prehistorical past, extending from the iron age and rise of indigenous African empires to the establishment of black colonial states and conquest by European empires. Vividly portrayed vignettes establish a pattern of mythic association between Janie Mae Crawford and Damballah Ouedo's wife, the West African Vodun sky and heaven goddess Ayida Ouedo.

Metaphors compare Janie's hair to the rainbow imagery associated with Ayida Ouedo. The townspeople see "her hair swingin' down her back" and they react as though "the great rope of black hair swinging to her waist and unraveling in the wind" were transforming into colorful rainbows; black contains every hue in the color spectrum (2). Just as celestial rainbows are Ayida Ouedo's signature, Janie's thick black hair is a motif that invokes Ayida Ouedo's altruistic spirit. When Janie cries, disconsolate over the "vision of Logan Killicks desecrating the pear tree," Nanny "[brushes] back the heavy hair from Janie's face" and says, "'Nanny wouldn't harm a hair uh yo' head,'" while she "sat rocking with the girl held tightly to her sunken breasts" (14). Then, "Nanny half sung, half sobbed a running chant-prayer over the head of the weeping girl," as "the long braids of her hair swung low" (14). Later, Joe Starks makes Janie wear a "head-rag," which "irks her endlessly" (55). Earlier, Joe saw a mule talker "brushing the back of his hand back and forth across the loose end of her braid ever so lightly so as to enjoy the feel of it without Janie knowing what he was doing" (55). Joe "felt like rushing forth with the meat knife and chopping off the offending hand" (55). Instead, he orders Janie "to tie up her hair around the store" (55).

In my syncretic allegorical interpretation, Janie Mae Crawford is a Vodun-Christian symbol. Her initials, J.M.C., evoke the Holy Family and refer in Roman Catholic theology to Joseph, Mary and Christ. Janie is a scion of Ayida Ouedo, creation goddess in West African Vodun theological cosmology. Janie explains to her confidante Phoeby Watson, "'Dey all useter call me 'Alphabet' 'cause so many people had done named me different names'" (9). Before Janie sees a photograph of herself, she exists in her own mind as an autonomous entity, a girl who has a distinctly independent existence. She is unable to recognize herself in the photo except by observation and deductive reasoning; her self-recognition and realization are painful: "'Aw, aw! Ah'm colored!'" (9). She is unaware that black is the one color that contains all of the other colors, hence black is an occult color that is a true symbol that stands for profundity, the universal, and the unknown. Her childhood nickname Alphabet elevates her status from orphaned girl who never saw her father and mother to affiliation with Ayida Ouedo the Vodun rainbow goddess. Since the English alphabet stretches out to form a string of twenty-six letters, the name Alphabet evokes a wide range of myriad phenomena. The prefix alpha- evokes the Genesaic beginning of the world, while the suffix -bet indicates the second letter of the alphabet, hence beta symbolizes continuity. Alphabet is a name that evokes a sinuous image of continuity, consecutive order, and flexibility. A rainbow is a vast, overarching peaceful thing of beauty that is adaptable and responsive to a wide range of terrestrial or aquatic environments. Janie's nickname Alphabet is a visual and conceptual metaphor that identifies Janie with Vodun celestial rainbow divinity Ayida Ouedo.

Janie Mae Crawford's love quest comprises an epic journey that evokes epochs in the history of Africa. Because Janie is a scion of Ayida Oueda, African Vodun creation goddess, *Their Eyes Were Watching God* analogizes her life to the family tree of the West African nations: "Janie saw her life like a great tree in leaf with the things suffered, things enjoyed, things done and undone. Dawn and doom was in the branches" (8). Metaphorically, "West Florida" is a synecdoche of West Africa (10). First, her marriage to Logan Killicks, a successful farmer, takes Janie to the brink of the iron-tool age in the fifth millennium B.C., when Africa made villages and domesticated the camel for trans-Sahara trade with Mediterranean cultures. Janie leaves Logan Killicks on a day when he rides his mule to town to barter for another plow mule. Her marriage to an ambitious and enterprising business-minded agriculturist catapults Janie into an upward spiral that gives her proprietary prosperity but exacts a toll, because their love nest is bereft of love. In her next marriage, her identity role as "Mrs. Mayor Starks" (110) evokes the rise of indigenous African empires. Janie's marriage to Mayor Joe Starks is a quasi poetic synecdoche that evokes the rise of strong black colonial city-states in fourteenth- and fifteenth-century Africa ("The years took all the fight out of Janie's face. For a while she thought it was gone from her soul. No matter what Jody did she said nothing . . . She got nothing from Jody but what money could buy") (76). Janie's love agony over their impoverished emotional life invokes the enslavement of the weaker by upwardly mobile forces of colonization under European empires in sixteenth-century Africa. Janie's impassioned diatribe to Joe Starks, held captive on his death-bed, evokes the tragic mass psychic suffering Africa withstood during the heyday of slave-trading kingdoms. Janie's shocking expression of hatred and resentment against Joe Starks's subjugation resonates in evocation of the far-reaching toll in human cruelty and suffering engendered in eighteenth- and nineteenth-century Africa by the Pan-African and transatlantic slave trade. Deren observes, "The first slave-trade shipment to Haiti was in 1510. The first slave revolt recorded was in 1522" (64). Significantly, Janie Mae Crawford finally finds happiness with a man of mixed African, European, and Caribbean ancestry whose pedigree spans the globe. Her courtship and marriage to Vergible "Tea Cake" Woods takes her on an eternal honeymoon trip that evokes the African diaspora in the New World and the ensuing liberation of colonized African nations that in bloody battles rebelliously vanquished oppressors at whose behest they suffered cruel acts of inhumanity at the hands of godless imperial armies. Throughout *Their Eyes Were Watching God*, Janie seeks to liberate herself from post-renaissance bourgeois materialism in affirmation of her Southern Baptist Christian roots in the American Deep South.

In my critical view, her quest for freedom may best be understood in terms of Vodun theological concepts. She marries Joe, "a citified, stylish dressed man" from Georgia (27), because "he spoke fur far horizon" (29). Joe Starks is a "Little Emperor" (88) whose ambitious founding in Florida of Eatonville evokes the rise of city-states in West Africa. During her marriage to Starks, Janie makes good on her wedding vows by playing the role of the woman her husband wants her to be, namely Erzulie Frieda, who adorns herself in "beautiful, expensive raiment" (Hurston, *Tell My Horse* 384). This marriage evokes the rise of West African imperialism in the fourteenth and fifteenth centuries. Janie resolves in good faith to conceal her true self, namely Ayida Ouedo, and she obediently dons the sumptuous clothes that Joe requires her to wear as the mayor's wife. She obeys Joe's order "to tie up her hair around the store" (55). Her self-abnegation suggests loyalty to her wedding vows and self-esteem, qualities that link her to Ayida Ouedo. Damballah and Ayida's "second name" of Ouedo indicates "a special quality of benevolence, respected authority, and prestige" (Deren 60). Paradoxically, her inner life[1] is as a slave to her husband's political ambitions, a condition of female bondage that evokes the West African institution of slavery in the eighteenth and nineteenth centuries. Joe Starks is like the beguiling serpent in the Garden of Eden, cursed by God to be a snake. Joe regains his dignity as an African-American entrepreneur and statesman who stands upright. Janie expected Joe would be "a bee for her bloom" (32), but he turns his "pretty doll-baby" into a mannequin-like house slave (29). At first, she is glad Joe is "kind of portly like rich white folks" (34). In Haitian Vodoun, white is the color associated with the major family of spirits known as Rada, which are guardians of morals and principles. Janie gives Joe a piece of her mind: "It's so easy to make y'self out to be God Almighty when you ain't got nothin' tuh strain against but women and chickens" (75). Dressed as Erzulie, she "watched a shadow of herself . . . prostrating itself before Jody" (77). Playing the role of Erzulie to his Legba Eshu is so out of character that her truth-telling self inadvertently derides his ability to produce offspring, and he feels betrayed: "He struck Janie with all his might. . . He didn't really hate Janie, but he wanted her to think so. He had crawled off to lick his wounds" (80-81). Joe falls ill from overwork that drains love from his soul, then life from his body. In the Old Testament Book of Genesis, God lays the serpent flat with a verbal kidney punch. When his kidneys fail, Joe suspects Janie has put a curse on him. He consults a Hoodoo "'faker'" or "'two-headed doctor'" (82, 83). Janie waits until he is dying before she renounces her marriage and repudiates her role as Erzulie. She avers, "'You ain't de Jody ah run off down de road wid. . . . But you wasn't satisfied wid me de way Ah was'" (86). Foreshadowing the demise of Tea Cake as his successor, Joe invokes the power of Shango, the Vodun god of thunder and lightning: "'Ah wish thunder and lightnin' would kill yuh!'" (86).

The arrival in the town store of Vergible "Tea Cake" Woods, an itinerant worker, evokes the African diaspora, the emancipation of slaves, and the liberation of Africans from government rule under European-domination in imperial European colonies. Tea Cake is a Creole, which in Spanish refers to an outsider of mixed European and black or American Indian ancestry. His nickname, Tea Cake, suggests his happy-to-lucky attitude as a rambling-shambling man and a professional gambler. The name Vergible Woods invokes Vodun spirit "Ogoun," whom Hurston ranks "in the [Voudoun] temple" with "Damballah" and "Legba" (*Tell My Horse* 382). Ogoun is linked to "sacred places" and "deep forests" (Owusu 38). His character is to be honest and vigilant. Initially, Janie thinks Vergible "Tea Cake" Woods is a gigolo because of his lackadaisical manner, which exemplifies a stock image of the war god: "Ogoun chews carelessly on a cigar and conducts himself like a true swordsman and lady-killer" (Owusu 38). To prove his sincerity to Janie, he avers, "'Ah'm de Apostle Paul tuh de Gentiles. Ah tells 'em and then agin Ah shows 'em'" (104). This biblical allusion evokes Paul's words to the elders: "Serving the Lord with all humility of mind, and with many tears, and temptations . . . I kept back nothing that was profitable unto you, but have shewed you and I have taught you publicly . . . Testifying both to the Jews, and also to the Greeks, repentance toward God, and faith toward our Lord Jesus Christ" (Acts 20:19-21). Vergible Woods modified his name by adding "Tea Cake," which is reminiscent of the way evangelist Paul changed his name from Saul when he decided to serve Christ. Dorsey observes, "Many of the [Voudoun] and Hoodoo practices contain elements of Christianity. St. Paul is often depicted wielding a sword" (68-69). As evangelist Paul served Jesus Christ, the Son of God, so, too, Tea Cake is an instrument of Ogoun, a stalwart liege of Damballah. Tea Cake and Janie's love shows that sinners caught in the throes of Shango's thunderous ferocity can be saved only by the overriding power of Damballah.

A visible paragon of heavy metal power and prestige, Ogoun serves Damballah. Ogoun is pictured with a machete, an ax, or an iron sword (Owusu 38).[2] Working through delicately etched detail, *Their Eyes Were Watching God* fuses Vodun and Christianity. Tea Cake's pal Motor Boat has a "face like a little black cherubim just from a church tower" (157) which alludes in the Bible to Judeo Christianity's passionate fight to defend innocence and purity from attack by evil: "Cherubims, and a flaming sword which turned every way, to keep the way of the tree of life" (Genesis 3:24). Although Motor Boat dies, *Their Eyes Were Watching God* illuminatingly portrays Vergible "Tea Cake" Woods as a Vodun Judeo Christian "flaming sword" and the "bee" that makes Janie feel a "remorseless sweet" pain that is "a marriage!" and "a revelation" (11). After Jane Mae Crawford returns home to recover from her ordeal and mourns the death of Tea Cake, she decides to celebrate Tea Cake's bravery during and after the hurricane. In the novel's concluding scene, Papa Legba invisibly makes the sun's hot rays blaze so that Ogoun's sword flashes shafts of light into the room: "Then Tea Cake came prancing around her where she was and the song of the sigh flew out of the window and lit in the top of the pine trees. Tea Cake, with the sun for a shawl" (193).The "kiss" of Tea Cake's "memory" and the "pictures of love and light against the wall"(193) evoke the "flaming sword" that will "keep the way of the tree of life" for the rest of Janie's life.

Vodun traditional belief is a pervasive element in Hurston's oeuvre. Ellease Southerland, Daphne Lamothe, Edward M. Pavlic, Derek Collins, and other scholars examine Hurston's *Their Eyes Were Watching God*, indicating the importance of traditional African Vodun and Haitian Voudoun beliefs vis-à-vis literature, ethnography, and modernity. Hurston's Vodun-Christianity fusion in *Jonah's Gourd Vine* depicts the protagonist's encounter with a sovereign river dweller in a symbolic drama that evokes Damballah Ouedo, the supreme Vodun spirit-god promoter of life. Damballah Ouedo energizes the material world, hence controls human regeneration, seasonal renewal in nature, and continuity in the universe. Hurston's description differentiates Vodun from Catholicism: "Damballah Ouedo is the supreme Mystere," and although the "picture that is bought of him is that of St. Patrick, he in no way resembles that Irish saint" (*Tell My Horse* 378).

Christians might associate *Jonah's Gourd Vine*'s river snake image with the biblical Garden of Eden. But Hurston regards the river occupant not primarily as a serpent debased by God for tempting humanity with forbidden knowledge but as a paragon of good health, beauty, truth, and committed love and loyalty. As a Vodun priest, Southern Baptist preacher John Buddy Pearson experiences the tragic implications of his transgression against the symbolic Damballah representative at the behest of erotic temptresses. While Janie Mae Crawford's social and economic rise contrasts sharply to Lucy's decline and death, Janie's Vodun love quest resurrects Lucy's Vodun-Christian devotion to a love that harmoniously conflates religious sanctions. Damballah's dynamism shapes Janie's undulating love quest and the hurricane episode in *Their Eyes Were Watching God*. Anna Lillios declares, "The hurricane is the most powerful symbol in the book" (89). Keith Cartwright quotes profusely to show that Hurston includes thunder and rain-bringer imagery in all her works. I am arguing that Hurston obliterates boundaries that define Africa and America as separate continents and adapts Vodun respect for nature and concepts of mounting and shape-changing. The African Vodun spirit-god Damballah protects Tea Cake, empowering him to restore Janie Mae Crawford, changing her from Mrs. Joe Starks–Erzulie Freida into Mrs. Vergible "Tea Cake" Woods–Ayida Ouedo. In the end, hurricane wind-spirit Oya and thunder god Shango turn Tea Cake into a nemesis; nevertheless, Damballah retains control over Janie's life.

Hurston adopts a dual religious perspective in her depiction of Janie's relationships with men. The biblically infused Old Testament and New Testament design of her depiction of Janie Mae Crawford's three marriages foregrounds Vodun traditional belief. After Nanny sees Johnny Taylor "lacerating" Janie with a forbidden "kiss" (12), she marries her granddaughter to a farmer who is redolent of Adam banished from Eden and condemned to live by the sweat of his brow, wearing the skins of brutes, and wallowing in the dust. Nanny justifies her decision, conflating Vodun and Christianity: "'De [black] woman is de mule uh de world so fur as Ah can see. Ah been prayin' fuh it tuh be different wid you. Lawd, Lawd, Lawd!'" (14). Nanny explains to Janie that freedom from the slave labor ethic of "'de white man'" is in Africa: "'Maybe it's some place way off in de ocean where de black man is in power'" (14). Janie Mae Crawford-Ayida Ouedo resents Nanny for taking "the biggest thing God ever made, the horizon" and pinching it into "'a little bit of a thing'" (89). Farmer Logan Killicks is a scion of Orunmila, the primeval Vodun "god of wisdom" (Fama 137, 208). Orunmila assures financial success by "cleansing the mind," even of sexual passion (Fama 54). Killicks prospers, because he reinvests profits into his farm of "sixty acres" (23, 31). He marries Janie because he plans to bequeath his estate to her, as befits Orunmila as patron god over "wealth and peace of mind" (Fama 60). A covenant blessed by Orunmila assures protection of family members (Fama 63). Janie languishes under Logan's regime of sacrifice. This marriage lasts until Janie Mae Crawford annuls her unconsummated marriage by rescinding her vows and then making good on her avowed intention to leave him on a day that is reminiscent of the inception of the Iron Age in West Africa in 400 B.C. Their verbal battles culminate in his threat to kill her with "dat ax" and he invokes the wrath of God on her and she resolves to leave him without compunction (32). Logan Killicks curses her after he hears her grievances and he realizes "you don't want me!" (32). Janie continues her duties, cleans house and cuts potatoes, until she attracts the attention of "a citified, stylish dressed man" from Georgia (27). Logan suffers from his loss of Janie, whose departure evokes Osun, Vodun goddess of love and beauty; Osun's "most severe punishment is her absence" (Curry 74). Janie Mae Crawford's idealistic view of marriage is rooted in Ayida Ouedo's undying loyalty to Damballah Ouedo.

Throughout *Their Eyes Were Watching God*, Hurston epitomizes Damballah as "the highest and most powerful of all the gods" (*Tell My Horse* 381) She depicts Janie as aspiring to the wedded bliss of Ayida Ouedo, the wife of Damballah Ouedo. But her contacts with Johnny Taylor, Logan Killicks, and Jody Starks are unsatisfactory infatuations, which make twists and turns in her incessantly thwarted yet overriding quest for love. Damballah is the motivating force that prompts Janie to reminisce over her married life with Tea Cake, whose love was like an embrace intertwining her dream with reality in a never-ending voyage in the jet stream of Ayida Ouedo and Damballah Ouedo's love: "Here was peace. She pulled in the horizon like a great fish-net. Pulled it from around the waist of the world and draped it over her shoulder. So much of life in its meshes! She called in her soul to come and see" (193). In "Dambala, of Damballah Ouedo (Pronounced Way-Doe)," Hurston states, "If a memory is great enough, other memories will cluster about it, and those in turn will bring their suites of memories to gather about this focal point, because perhaps, they are all scattered parts of the one thing like Plato's concept of the perfect thing" (*Tell My Horse* 378). Janie Mae Crawford-Ayida Ouedo and Vergible "Tea Cake" Woods-Ogoun incarnate nature deities that represent love and conflict in the context of passionate love that a transatlantic hurricane transforms into unending spiritual love by the influence of transoceanic spirit-god Damballah Ouedo working through deities Shango and his wife, Oya.

Janie Mae Crawford's epic quest for unconditional love in the face of adversity is reminiscent of the defeated Trojan armies fleeing from victorious imperial Greek armies and founding the Roman Empire at Latium in Virgil's *The Aeneid*.[3] Sea imagery at the beginning of *Their Eyes Were Watching God* evokes the transatlantic voyage of West Africans in slave ships to southeastern America and the Caribbean. The novel's first words are poetic: "Ships at a distance have every man's wish on board. For some they come in with the tide. For others they sail forever on the horizon, never out of sight, never landing until the Watcher turns his eyes away in resignation, his dreams mocked to death by Time" (1). Moonless nights and windless waters on the Guinea coast allow captive black men to get their wish to return "with the tide" to Africa. The image of the archetypal Watcher evokes African men on slave ships who perish at sea and also those who survive the endless sea voyage yet refuse to accept the landing as their true destination. Women keep their dreams because "The dream is the truth. Then they act and do things accordingly. So the beginning of this was a woman and she had come back from burying the dead" (1). Readers who are familiar with the Negro folktales collected posthumously in Hurston's *Every Tongue Got to Confess* recognize that Hurston uses the African storytelling convention of the flashback such that *Their Eyes Were Watching God* is a novel modeled on the African preacher tale genre, as John Lowe suggests in observing that "Janie Mae Crawford finds the 'pulpit' Lucy Potts Pearson always deserved" (156). Janie resembles Liza in "Testimony," which begins "Dere wuz once uh woman who b'longded to de church an' she uster git up an' tell de greatest experience of anybody. No matter whut nobody said, she always carried it past 'em. So one Sunday when de Love-Feast wuz red hot, she got up and said: 'Brothers and Sisters, I jes been tuh heben in mah vision. . . An' Gawd wuz in de beanpatch pickin' beans'" (22). "Testimony" ends, "An' dat broke up de meetin' in uh fight" (23). Provocatively, *Their Eyes Were Watching God*'s opening passages lay claim to a limitless domain that intertwines sea voyages with men's wishes, history with Time, and the dream with truth. This epic prologue introduces Janie's Vodun-Christian African-American epic story about a woman-in-love who now returns from a big lake where "sodden" and "bloated" bodies with "their eyes flung open in judgment" needed burial after hurricane winds subsided (1). Epic simile evokes the hurricane's aftermath, "The sun was gone, but he had left his footprints in the sky" (1). Nature imagery links together Vodun theology and the transatlantic hurricane caused by rising temperatures on the Sahara Desert combined with the hot air spun by turbulent wind and condensation creating a jet stream, which is Damballah Ouedo's signature. Thus "horizon" refers to the troposphere between earth's surface and the stratosphere, which is Ayida Ouedo's realm, where weather fronts and rainbows form. Her use of the scientific method to record her empirical observations of Haitian Voudoun rituals and practices prepared her to depict the Florida hurricane as a transatlantic phenomenon that may be comprehended in terms of West African Vodun as a monotheist religion based on reverent worship of and respect for nature. The hurricane episode conflates Christianity and Vodun by evoking Christian faith in God in the context of powerful Vodun spirit-gods with a visible presence in nature.

Hurston stresses that Africans worship Damballah Ouedo as a creation divinity. The story of Damballah and Ayida Ouedo's transatlantic transport of Vodun from Africa to the Caribbean parallels Oya's and Shango's destructive power to move sand-wind-thunder-rainstorms from the Sahara to the Americas. Her credible depiction of Moses as a Hoodoo priest in *Moses, Man of the Mountain* includes a plausible and scientifically astute account of how Moses led the Hebrews along an ebb tide path that parted the Red Sea when he summoned "the east wind" (191). In her capacity as a folklore specialist, she fuses Damballah with the rod as a symbol of Moses in the Old Testament and the crucifix as a symbol of Christ in the New Testament. "Damballah with the subtle wisdom and powers represented by the snake is to the African something of a creator, if not actively, certainly The Source. His color is white. His woman is Aida Ouedo. His signature is the ascending snakes on a rod or a crucifix. He is the fourth in the order of the service being preceded by (1) Papa Legba, opener of gates (opportunities), (2) Loco Attison, Mystère of work and knowledge, (3) Mah-lah-sah, the guardian of the doorsill. None of these are so important as Damballah" (*Zora Neale Hurston: Folklore, Memoirs, and Other Writings* 382).

Their Eyes Were Watching God introduces the theme of metamorphic transformation in the image of working people whose skin is "occupied" by "mules and other brutes" during the day. But by night their "skins" feel "powerful and human," and they become "lords" who pass "nations through their mouths" and sit "in judgment" (1). The novel pursues this pointed statement of Vodun folk belief in shape-changing in its oscillating plot design as Janie Mae Crawford adapts to the milieus provided by Nanny, Logan Killicks, Joseph "Jody" Starks, and Vergible "Tea Cake" Woods. She is at a threshold where she, as a Christian, tells a Vodun love story to "Mouth-Almighty" (4) to account for why she is not the jilted Annie Tyler and Tea Cake is not the jilter Who Flung. Pheoby Watson observes, "'Sam say most of 'em goes to church so they'll be sure to rise in Judgment'" (6). The atmosphere for Janie's "self-revelation" suggests the post-mortem incarnation of Papa Legba. Legba as a young man is the sun but after sunset Guedé is the "night sun" god of the "underworld" (Deren 102). Legba is god of life, but death transfigures Legba into Guedé, who is called "Rising Sun" (Deren 102). Hurston refers to "Brave Guedé" as "messenger of all the gods" (*Tell My Horse* 434). While Legba "was once Lord of Life," Guedé is "Lord of Resurrection" (Deren 102). Dolan Hubbard holds that Janie articulates the "communal language" of "the black church"; he argues that "Janie's sermon becomes a poetry of affirmation" (112-113). If Janie were to preach a sermon, the moral would be that her twenty-year marriage to Joe Starks was really servitude to Mammon, a Christian derogation for material wealth, at the expense of love. Her message is that she is blessed by a love inspirited, indeed made possible, by the passion of Jesus Christ commingled with the power of Damballah Ouedo.

Their Eyes Were Watching God reprises Hurston's veneration for Damballah Ouedo by adapting the belief in spirit-gods inhabiting certain places and exerting a spiritual influence on a person. Specifically, Hurston evokes the invisible presence of Damballah Ouedo in her portrayal of Janie's third husband such that Damballah Ouedo's presence is manifested in Tea Cake's actions. The influence of Damballah is a barely perceptible undercurrent, coupled with the overarching love-engendered trajectory of Janie as the wife of Tea Cake as inspirited by Damballah. Hurston transforms into art her anthropological investigations so that her depiction of Vodun theology in *Their Eyes Were Watching God* is at once imaginative and realistic, particularly in the hurricane episode. Sarah Ford argues, "The storm actually questions any human agency; the chaos overturns basic human attempts to order the world and questions human constructions of reality . . . [T]he hurricane is not in conflict with the rest of the narrative . . . as Janie gains the power to tell her own story not despite the storm but through that very experience" (408). Lillios shows that Hurston drew on "her own fearful experience" of the 1929 hurricane and the "awesome power of the 1953 storm," stressing that Hurston "drew on the details of the West Indian hurricane of September 1928," which was "one of the most powerful on record" (90). Lillios observes that the hurricane "propels" Janie to "move from the muck" to "a brave new world" (89).

In Vodun worship, drums summon the loa spirits. Shango, god of thunder, determines the fatal destiny of Tea Cake, who sacrifices his life to save Janie's life. The hurricane fatally attacks Tea Cake's love for Janie. When Tea Cake uses "his knife" (166) to kill a rabid dog that bit him, symbolically he ends his own life because Ogoun's totem animal is a dog.[4] When the "massive built dog" that was "shivering and growling" perched atop "a cow swimming" to a fill (165-66) bites him, he reverts back to his Vodun defined identity as archetypal warrior. Vodun thunder god Shango, Ogoun's rival, divests Tea Cake of his identity as a lover. Tea Cake "opened his knife as he dived," but the rabid dog "managed to bite Tea Cake high up on the cheek-bone once. Then Tea Cake finished him to the bottom to stay there" (166). But Shango wins. Shango's sacred animal, "the ram," pounds the earth with hooves of fire" (Herskovits, *Dahomean Narrative* 64-65). During rabies' four-week incubation, Tea Cake is drafted into "a small army," ordered to help "clear the wreckage" and "bury the dead" (170). He is a mortally wounded soldier of love defeated by hurricane forces unleashed by Shango and Shango's wife, Oya, the Vodun goddess of rain and wind, and a gatekeeper of the cemetery.

During the armed face-off Janie observes that Tea Cake is no longer himself: "'Tea Cake, you'se sick. You'se takin' everything in de way Ah don't mean it'" (182). Shango and Oya changed him into an iconic rabid canine image of Ogoun that moved toward her with "a queer loping gate, swinging his head from side to side and his jaws clenched in a funny way" (183). Blindly, he points a pistol at Janie, because he relives his battle in the hurricane, seeing Janie as the dog that threatened their lives: "Janie . . . saw the quick motion of taking aim and heard the click. Saw the ferocious look in his eyes and went mad with fear as she had done in the water that time. . . Tea Cake . . . paid no more attention to the pointing gun than if it were Janie's dog finger" (184). Before Janie met Tea Cake, "she had been whipped like a cur dog, and run off down a back road after things" (89). When she aims at him, she is that dog again, because she wants him to stay with her as a living body, and he aims his pistol at her thinking she is the rabid dog. Their judgment is unequivocal. Their use of firearms and lead bullets in self-defense is consistent with testimonial procedures in "Nigerian courts," where "witnesses are sworn in with their hand touching a piece of iron" (Dorsey 16). Their love oath is as definitive as death triggered by Shango and Oya's destructive ravages.

Cartwright observes that *Jonah's Gourd Vine* "opens to Oya's storming," and *Their Eyes Were Watching God* "commences with invocations of the Oya-swept dead" (752). Oya's husband Shango is the Vodun god of light-ning and thunder and the lord of fire and the drum that coincides with the wrath of the Judeo-Christian God of Holy Scripture. During the storm a Vodun drum imitates Shango's thunder, which resonates with Christian over-tones: "Stew Beef vibrating the drum head near the edge with his fingers. By morning Gabriel," named after the angel appearing to Virgin Mary in the Annunciation, "was playing the deep tones in the center of the drum" (158). Then Motor Boat compares Shango and Oya to the cruelty of an archetypal slave master: "A big burst of thunder and lightning that trampled over the roof of the house. . . Motor looked up in his angel-looking way and said, 'Big Massa draw him chair upstairs'" (159).

Contrapuntally, personification of "old Okechobee" as a "monster" that "began to roll in his bed" poetically indicates Oya's rising waves of wind and rain. Oya is the wind goddess who resides in lakes like Florida's Okechobee. She is one of Shango's three wives. The African-American Christians are impervious to the storm's heightening danger and do not give the appropriate respect by evacuating the area because New World conditioning prompts them to follow the white master and to "wait on the mercy of [his] Lord." They see Okeechobee as a monstrous lake that "the bossman" will "have ...stopped before morning." Janie Mae Crawford reveals unconscious knowledge of Shango when she rebukes Motor Boat, who invokes the Judeo-Christian God: "Big Massa draw him chair upstairs." Reverently, Janie Mae Crawford announces, "Ole Massa is doin' His work now. Us oughta keep quiet" (158). In striking contrast to Motor Boat's high regard for the Judeo-Christian God—"Big Massa," Janie Mae Crawford respects the "work" of "Ole Massa," the ancient Vodun thunder god Shango. Her veneration for the power of Shango to make the lake into a "senseless monster" (159) foreshadows the rabies' displacement of Tea Cake's psyche, a symbolic possession.

Commensurate with the storm's chaos and cacaphony, Hurston depicts Shango and Oya wrenching Tea Cake away from the benevolent protection of Damballah afforded by Janie's love. Tea Cake-Ogoun is imaged as a man who is clinging to a "cypress tree" and as a "tin roof" hanging from "the branches by electric wires" with "the wind" swinging it "back and forth like a mighty ax" (164-65). Meanwhile, Damballah is imaged as "a large rattle-snake," which is "stretched full length with his head in the wind" (165). Paradoxically, the rattle auditory image implicates Damballah as the power-house that energizes Shango and Oya. The rattling sound connects onomato-poeically to the sounds of thunder, lightning, rain, and wind. Tree and iron imagery evoke Esu-Elegbara and Ogoun.

Vodun *orisha* are "aspects of God, forces of nature or the universe viewed from different angles . . . specialized forms of the Supreme God" (Curry 64). In scientific terms, hurricanes originate in Africa when hot air rising above the Sahara Desert clashes with high winds carrying moisture inland from the West African Guinea coast, spawning storms. In *Their Eyes Were Watching God*, Damballah Ouedo's transatlantic jet stream flowing at high velocity has transported the storm from Africa to Florida, to Lake Okechobee from the Sahara Desert. Historically, the westward trajectory of West African slave ships and of the culture of the African captives parallels the path of the weather system that brings storms from Africa to America. Seemingly, Oya's wind renders the symbolic Vodun snake guardian innocuous, like a wilted vine. Tea Cake yells to Janie, "'De snake won't bite yuh. He skeered tuh go intuh a coil. Skeered he'll be blowed away'" (165). The dramatic irony is brilliant in evoking a slight withdrawal of Damballah's power to save Tea Cake from falling immediately into the clutches of Shango and Oya. Oya succeeds in unseating Damballah. Just as Christ was crucified and God did not prevent it, so Tea Cake fights the storm without aid from the Vodun god that is the "great source" (Hurston, *Tell My Horse* 381). Hurston uses natural references to depict the hurricane as a transatlantic phenomenon that may be comprehended in terms of an African and American collaboration that turns on forces that are divinely activated.

Hurston hails Damballah Ouedo as "the great and the pure" who "looks after peace and love in the home" (*Tell My Horse* 434). Tea Cake's battles with a rabid dog and Janie's confrontation with a dog-zombie are synecdoches of the hurricane as manifestations of Shango and Oya's destructive power. The hurricane interferes with Tea Cake and Janie's marriage. Damballah and Ayida Ouedo are transcendent divinities, present in streams of water and air, hence imbue their devotees, i.e., husbands and wives, with the continuity of eternal love. We recall Tea Cake and Janie's driving tour along the strand on a sunshiny day invokes Osun, the Nigerian river sacred to Osun (Oshún), the goddess of love. When Vergible "Tea Cake" Woods takes Janie Mae Crawford to the Florida Everglades, he swims powerfully amid the tempestuous waters of a hurricane, battling to save Janie-Ayida Ouedo from succumbing to the machinations of arch villains Shango and Oya, the Vodun spirit-gods that transform a whirlwind romance into an exalted love that transcends the storm.

The social and economic rise to prominence of Janie Mae Crawford contrasts sharply to the decline and death of Lucy Potts Pearson. Yet, Janie's mythic love quest recuperates Lucy's tragic devotion to a forbidden love that undermines societal structure in daring to travel across class boundaries. As Lowe observes, *Jonah's Gourd Vine* "provided Hurston a great rehearsal for the issues she would raise in her masterwork, *Their Eyes Were Watching God*. In some ways, Janie's story resurrects Lucy, now free to go forward and preach the great sermon that her social role in the earlier novel denies her. Janie, child-free, financially secure, leaves one husband, buries two others, and finds the 'pulpit' Lucy always deserved" (156). Similarly, Meisenhelder observes, "As in *Jonah's Gourd Vine*, Hurston also focused on 'family matters' in *Their Eyes Were Watching God*, examining in greater detail models of black male and female identity and the larger social worlds they both reflect and shape. . . The discursive difficulties Hurston faced in telling this story were perhaps even greater than those she faced in writing *Jonah's Gourd Vine,* for the powerful black woman Janie becomes resists oppression not merely by haunting her husband after her death as Lucy does, but much more directly, 'killing' one man with words and another with a gun" (62).

But *Their Eyes Were Watching God* is an even more ambitious undertaking than has hitherto been supposed.

Consciously or unconsciously, Hurston has structured *Their Eyes Were Watching God* into a pattern that coincides with West African history. In this historical allegory, the life of Janie Crawford, and especially her marriages to three men of different walks of life and cultural backgrounds, symbolize stages in West Africa's history, extending from the prehistorical past to farming and domestication of cattle around the fifth millennium B.C., to the expansion of agricultural productivity by ironworking technology about 400 B.C., to the development of modest "city-states," to the "domestication of the camel" that made possible "cross-Sahara trade with Mediterranean culture," to the rise of indigenous African empires beginning with the Ghana Empire in the eighth century A.D., followed by the Sosso Empire, Mali Empire, Songhai Empire, and Ashanti Empire, to the rise of "strong city-states (Ife, Bono, and Benin) in the fourteenth and fifteenth centuries," to the colonization under European empires in the sixteenth century, to emergence of "slave-trading kingdoms" in the eighteenth and nineteenth centuries, to the transatlantic slave trade to the African diaspora in the New World, and finally, to the "post-independence era in which the current nations were formed" ("West Africa"). Simultaneously, *Their Eyes Were Watching God* establishes patterns of mythic association between the fictional character Janie Crawford and the pantheon of West African goddesses, especially Damballah Ouedo's wife, sky goddess Ayida Ouido.

Janie Mae Crawford recounts the transmogrifications of her life brought about by her three marriages, which Hurston portrays with symbolic references to African cosmological theology. On an elemental level, agriculturist Killicks Logan is reminiscent of Vodun god Ofun, whose element is earth. Joe emulates Olorun, the owner of heaven whose element is fire, exemplified when Mayor Starks ceremoniously uses great pomp and circumstance to erect a town lamp. Significantly, Janie tells Phoeby her story ensconced in the house provided, and the town built, by Joe Starks-Olorun. Damballah blesses Tea Cake-Ogoun, a warrior of love who emulates transatlantic air and water currents when he woos, wins, and holds Janie's love in a continuous flow of romantic rendezvous. Yet, Olorun "presides over the universe" (Fama 266). Olorun is the invisible creator deity, the cosmic creation god of the universe. Her lecture to Phoeby repudiates the biblical archetypal image of woman. Janie, unlike Eve, fulfills her desire to partake exclusively of the tree of life. Janie emulates a prelapsarian Eve when she scornfully rebukes those who put their trust in facile words: "It's uh known fact, Phoeby, you got tuh go there tuh know there . . . Two things everybody's got tuh do fuh theyselves. They got tuh go tuh God, and they got tuh find out about livin' fuh theyselves" (192). In a novelistic tour de force, Hurston depicts Janie as a Southern Baptist wife who is obedient to her husband(s). But as a West

African-American woman emblematizing Ayida Ouedo she is in a state of grace, hence in a natural condition of blissful obedience both to Damballah and to the God of Holy Scripture.

Hurston creates and governs the textual universe of *Jonah's Gourd Vine* and *Their Eyes Were Watching God*, which makes possible critical explorations of the subtextual domain of meaning. Her novels crystallize and amplify the anthropology in her nonfiction writings, because the novel genre is innately multidimensional and commodious enough to accommodate theological resonances. In *Jonah's Gourd Vine*, the protracted separation of John Buddy from his natural father, the alienation that keeps him from having a good relationship with his stepfather, and his unresolved pity and hatred toward his mother ("the welts on her face and body hurt her") lead irremediably to his anger against both Damballah and Jonah's God, causing his instinctual desire to slay a spirit god of maleness, and to his defiant obsessive compulsive behavior patterns (12). John Buddy Pearson, like Jonah, is born into an incorrigible world. *Jonah's Gourd Vine* has four homiletic chapters. First, John hides from God, because he is happy with Lucy. Next, he is cast adrift and swept into marriage to Hattie. Then, John "prayed for Lucy's return," and finally, "God had answered with Sally" (200). He knows that he likes being married to Sally because he wants "Faith and no questions asked" (200). He resembles the Ninevites, who "cannot discern between their right hand and their left hand" (Holy 685 Jonah 4:11). God rewards Jonah for pitying the gourd, which symbolizes the community. But men who "observe lying vanities forsake their own mercy" (Holy 684 Jonah 2:8). Consequently, Jonah "wished in himself to die" (Jonah 4:8). The worm that smites Jonah's protective gourd symbolizes this death-wish. Redolent of the Vodun scion of Damballah that he took away from the river of life, John Buddy Pearson dies, still fighting, more heroically than ever, to save his soul: "He drove on but half-seeing the railroad from looking inward" (200). John Buddy Pearson personifies a blind life force, and he dies, in the same way that Janie Mae Crawford lives, in the line of duty, trying to understand, in order to be able to forgive himself and others. Janie tells Phoeby Watson, "It was not death she feared. It was misunderstanding. If they made a verdict that Janie didn't want Tea Cake and wanted him dead, then that was a real sin and a shame. It was worse than murder" (188). In adopting the perspective of Olodumare, a water-spirit creator divinity that is vast and mighty enough to spring into being without parentage, Janie Mae Crawford empathizes with Vergible "Tea Cake" Woods as a Christ figure who died as a martyr to the power of adversity to inflict suffering upon humankind.

Throughout *Their Eyes Were Watching God*, Janie Mae Crawford seeks to liberate herself from the bourgeois materialism of her traditional Christian roots in the postcolonialist American Deep South. Her quest for freedom may be understood in terms of Vodun theological concepts. Nanny's upbringing taught her a Christian lifestyle. Janie learned to respect her elders. Nana Buluku is a "maternal deity representing female courage, grand knowledge, and power" (Dorsey 198). Obatala, an androgynous Vodun deity, is the "creator god and goddess" and the "embodiment of clarity, heavenly peace, and purity" (Dorsey 17). Her grandmother Nanny is a matriarchal shaper who marries Janie off to a hard-working elderly farmer and Janie makes do with the constraints imposed on her freedom by a stable, secure situation. She resolves to "tend her grandmother's grave" (89). Dorsey observes, "The tradition of matriarchy and feminine power in the African diasporic religions is strong. Some even believe the supreme creator divinity of the Yoruba, Oludumare, to be a female. However, with goddesses like Yemonja, Oya, Oba, Osun, and others, the importance of women in the cosmology and the culture cannot be denied" (6).

At Janie and Logan's wedding reception, Nanny serves foods pleasing to Vodun "god of wisdom" Orunmila (Fama 137, 208): "cakes" and "rabbit and chicken" (21). Janie's marriage to Killicks is redolent of primitive living conditions in West Africa in the fifth millennium B.C. The Vodun spirit presiding over their marriage is Orunmila, "Witness to God's creations" and "Consultant-General in heaven" (Fama 137).

Their Eyes Were Watching God is a revelation of how theological pluralism, the religions and ideologies of both masters and slaves (regardless of color), provide a societal context for this story of a woman whose history has homiletic and epic overtones. The novel that Hurston gives us is an African panegyric. Through her depiction of character and her use of imagery and symbolism, Hurston seamlessly melds together Vodun and Christianity, so impeccably that the seams do not show, much in the same way that Vodun and Christianity operate in African-American life: life and art mirror one another. The flawless realism in her portrayal of African-American life is evocative so that she achieves narrative fluidity and incisiveness that allow for a truly revelatory art of the novel. The theological pluralism of Vodun and Christianity that resides at the heart of African-American culture informs the artistic quest of Zora Neale Hurston to reveal her spiritual vision of a theological integration that eclipses racial discrimination.

The film adaptation *Their Eyes Were Watching God* takes poetic license in ways that highlight the novel's foundation in West African Vodun theology. The movie exploits the visual poetry in scenic aquatic settings that imbue local color background camera shots that foreground Janie with a mythic resonance that codes water as an elemental Vodun motif. Her ecstatic moment of freedom when she sounds the depths of her soul after she learns that Nanny has betrothed her to Logan Killicks invokes Oba, the Santeria goddess who resides in lakes. Later, Janie fondles the white handkerchief that Joe Starks handed to her as a sign of his admiration, which invokes Obatala, known as the "king of the white cloth, and thus represents divine cleanliness"; furthermore, Obatala is the "creator god and goddess" and is the "embodiment of clarity, heavenly peace, and purity" (Dorsey 17). Finally, when Tea Cake takes Janie to the Florida Everglades, her deep water immersion invokes Yemonja, the Yoruban and Santeria goddess of the sea, as well as Oya, the Vodun goddess of lightning and tornado winds. Earlier, Janie and Tea Cake's driving tour along the strand on a sunshiny day invokes Osun, the Nigerian river sacred to Osun, the goddess of love.

Vodun color symbolism gives special meaning to the film sequence in which Joe gives Janie his white handkerchief. The chaste symbol of the white handkerchief is paired with, and cancels out, the reasoned-out act of abandonment that precedes it. The symbol of the white handkerchief is coupled with the chivalrous way Joe presents it to Janie. The white handkerchief is a Judeo-Christian symbol of Janie's marriage, which coincides with Jonah's being saved from drowning when God puts him into the body of a whale. Although Janie gains freedom from an odious marriage to Logan Killicks, the legally disjointed pattern of the precipitous way she extricates herself does not bode well for her ensuing marriage to Joe. Joe Starks liberates Janie from an untenable marriage to a man old enough to be her grandfather, a man for whom wedlock sanctions him to be a slave master to his wife. Ironically, during Joe's twenty-year marriage to Janie, the wheel of fate turns, and as Joe ages, he comes to be a twin to Logan, the man from whom he rescued Janie. This circular pattern carries moral and spiritual implications related to the Book of Jonah, which ends with God acknowledging Jonah's humility as a wise man amid worldly men.

In the end, Janie Mae Crawford enunciates the conclusions she has drawn from her experiences as a wedded woman. "Love is lak de sea. It's uh movin; thing, but still and all, it takes it shape from the de shore it meets, and it's difference with every shore" (191). Her lecture to Pheoby repudiates the biblical archetypal image of woman. Janie, unlike Eve, tries to circumnavigate the tree of knowledge of good and evil. Janie is a prelapsarian Eve. In a novelistic *tour de force* Hurston depicts Janie as a West African Vodun woman who, unlike Eve, is in a state of nature, hence in a human condition of blissfull obedience to God. This dutiful obedience to the Judeo-Christian lesson in Genesis is rewarded, as indicated in her avowal of belief in eternal life. Vodun *orisha* are "aspects of God, forces of nature or the universe viewed from different angles, specialized forms of the Supreme God" (Curry 64). At the highest level, Hurston creates and governs the textual universe of these two novels, which makes possible critical explorations of their achievable range of meanings. Thus her novels absorb and redirect the anthropology in her nonfiction writings because the novel genre is inherently capacious and voluminous enough to retain theological resonances. Her artistic consciousness emulates Olokun. Olokun is the *orisha* of the depths of the ocean in Santeria and Yoruba theology. Olokun is associated with the "collective

unconscious mind." Both in "physical impression" and "symbolic extensions," Olokun shows a merging (indistinctness) of form that speaks of "pre-
conscious matters" (Curry 75). *Jonah's Gourd Vine* merges river deity Damballah Ouedo with a guardian river snake to evoke in modern metaphors the
primitive and the postmodern identification of the divinity with the divinity's
guard. *Their Eyes Were Watching God* merges together celestial *orisha* Ayida Ouedo with the lower world *loa* Erzulie Frieda in Hurston's portrayal of
Janie Mae Crawford. In paralleling Janie Mae Crawford's three husbands
with epochs in Africa's history and also with major Vodun deities, Hurston
enriches *Their Eyes Were Watching God* by making concrete elements of
realism form a multidimensional symbolism that embraces Vodun Judeo
Christian theological values that harmonize Africa with America.

In "How It Feels to Be Colored," Hurston declares, "No one on earth ever
had a greater chance for glory. The world to be won and nothing to be lost"
(114). *Jonah's Gourd Vine* tells the story of a colored man for whom everything goes wrong; it is a scathing indictment, not of that man, but of the far-
reaching repercussions of the institution of slavery. *Their Eyes Were Watching God* is a revelation that Janie tells Phoebe about a colored woman, but it
is also an aesthetically veiled epic journey from prehistoric West Africa to
post-colonial America. Zora Neale Hurston stands close to Mark Twain, who
advanced the American realist novel genre with his conflation of adult and
children's perspectives in *The Adventures of Tom Sawyer* and his use of
American dialect in *Adventures of Huckleberry Finn.* Just as Twain depicts
the troubled soul of antebellum American civilization, so Hurston takes a
grass roots novelistic approach in her theologically inspired descent into the
soul of America. At the pinnacle of the Harlem Renaissance era, when most
Americans remained as yet unaware of the depths of African Americans'
retention of West African Vodun beliefs and practices dovetailing with Judeo-Christian theology, Hurston blazes a path that restores the theological
heritage of the African American.

NOTES

1. Barbara Johnson "discusses how Janie's strategy of separating her inner from her outer
self during her marriage to Joe empowers her to speak" (see Cassidy 262; Jordan 211-212).

2. Erik Curren attributes Tea Cake's decision not to accept a ride out of the muck to "the
complacency of those who think that their folk heritage protects them from participating in the
prejudices and attachment to hierarchy associated with white America" and that the title characters "should have been watching the material world, and following the example of the
Indians, animals, and Bahamians who are in closer touch with nature and who know when to
get out," but they dally because "their eyes are, and have been for too long, watching God—the
mythic principle of hierarchical power" (413). Jennifer Jordan describes *Their Eyes Were
Watching God* as a "cautionary tale, warning the black community against being seduced by
the appeal of white, middle-class values" (see Cassidy 268; Jordan 108).

3. Phillis Wheatley (b. 1753, Senegal or Gambia, d. 1784, Boston), the first African-American poet, like Hurston, read Vergil's *The Aeneid* as well as other Greek and Latin classics and the Bible. She was named after the ship, called *The Phillis*, which brought her across the Atlantic Ocean. She was purchased by John Wheatley, a wealthy Boston merchant, as a gift to his wife, Susanna. Their daughter Mary taught her to read by age nine. Phillis Wheatley wrote *Poems on Subjects Religious and Moral* (London 1773) and was emancipated shortly thereafter. Wheatley received letters of recognition from Voltaire, George Washington, and many other admirers of her poetical works. Her anthologized and widely taught poem on slavery, "On Being Brought from Africa to America" concludes, "Remember, Christians, Negroes, black as Cain, / May be refin'd, and join th' angelic train."

4. Thomas Cassidy observes, "Tea Cake's transformation after the dog bite does not seem to be the result of a totally foreign element invading his psyche as much as an acceleration of forces already evident in his personality before the storm" (264).

WORKS CITED

Brandon, George. *Santeria from Africa to the New World: The Dead Sell Memories: Blacks in the Diaspora*. Bloomington: Indiana University Press, 1997.

Burris, Andrew. "The Browsing Reader. Review of *Jonah's Gourd Vine*." *Critical Essays on Zora Neale Hurston*. Edited by Gloria L. Cronin. New York: G. K. Hall, 1998. 35-36.

Cartwright, Keith. "'To Walk with the Storm': Oya as the Transformative 'I' of Zora Neale Hurston's Afro-Atlantic Callings." *American Literature* 78, no. 4 (December 2006): 741-67.

Cassidy, Thomas. "Janie's Rage: The Dog and the Storm in *Their Eyes Were Watching God*." *CLA Journal: A Quarterly of the College Language Association* 36, no. 3 (March 1993): 260-69.

Collins, Derek. "The Myth and Ritual of Ezili Freda in Hurston's *Their Eyes Were Watching God*." *Western Folklore* 55, no. 2 (Spring 1996): 137-54.

Cronin, Gloria L., ed. *Critical Essays on Zora Neale Hurston*. New York: G. K. Hall, 1998.

Curren, Erik. "Should Their Eyes Have Been Watching God? Hurston's Use of Religious Experience and Gothic Horror." *African American Review* 29, no. 1 (1995): 17-24.

Curry, Mary Cuthrell. *Living Gods of Haiti*. Kingston: McPherson, 1970.

Deren, Maya. *Divine Horsemen: Living Gods of Haiti*. New York: Vanguard, 1953.

Desmangles, Leslie G. *The Faces of the Gods: Vodou and Roman Catholicism in Haiti*. Chapel Hill and London: University of North Carolina Press, 1992.

Dorsey, Lilith. *Voodoo and Afro-Caribbean Paganism*. Foreword by Isaac Bonewits. New York: Citadel Press, Kensington Publishing Group, 2005.

Fama, Chief Àiná Adéwálé-Somadhi. *Fundamentals of the Yorùbá Religion Òrìsà Worship*. San Bernardino: Ilé Òrúnmìlà Publications, 1993.

Ford, Sarah. "Necessary Chaos in Hurston's *Their Eyes Were Watching God*." *CLA Journal: A Quarterly of the College Language Association* 43, no. 4 (June 2000): 407-19.

Gates, Henry Louis, Jr. Afterword. *Seraph on the Sewanee: A Novel*. 1948. By Zora Neale Hurston. Foreword by Hazel V. Carby. New York: Harper Perennial, 1991.

Herskovits, Melville J. *The American Negro: A Study in Racial Crossing*. Bloomington: Indiana University Press, 1938.

———. *Cultural Dynamics*. Abridged from *Cultural Anthropology*. 1947. Preface by Joseph H. Greenberg. New York: Alfred A. Knopf, 1964.

Holloway, Joseph E., ed. *Africanisms in American Culture*. Bloomington and Indianapolis: Indiana University Press, 1990.

Holy Bible. Old and New Testaments. King James Version. New York: Books, 1951.

Hubbard, Dolan. "'... Ah said Ah'd save de text for you'": Recontextualizing the Sermon to Tell (Her)story in Zora Neale Hurston's *Their Eyes Were Watching God*." *Critical Essays on Zora Neale Hurston*. Edited by Gloria L. Cronin. New York: G. K. Hall, 1998. 100-113.

Hughes, Langston. *The Big Sea*. New York: Hill and Wang, 1940.

Hurston, Zora Neale. *Jonah's Gourd Vine*. 1934. Edited by Henry Louis Gates, Jr. Foreword by Rita Dove. New York: HarperPerennial, 1990.

———. *Moses, Man of the Mountain*. 1939. Foreword by Deborah E. McDowell. New York: HarperPerennial, 1991.

———. *Seraph on the Suwanee*. 1948. Foreword by Hazel V. Carby. Afterword by Henry Louis Gates, Jr. New York: HarperPerennial, 2008.

———. "Songs of Worship to Voodoo Gods." *Zora Neale Hurston: Folklore, Memoirs, and Other Writings*. New York: Library of America, 1995. 533-55.

———. *Tell My Horse*. *Zora Neale Hurston: Folklore, Memoirs, and Other Writings*. New York: Library of America, 1995. 376-97.

———. "Testimony." *Every Tongue Got to Confess: Negro Folk-Tales from the Gulf States*. Edited by Carla Kaplan. New York: HarperCollins, 2001. 22-23.

———. *Their Eyes Were Watching God*. Foreword by Mary Helen Washington. Afterword by Henry Louis Gates, Jr. New York: J. P. Lippincott, 1937; Perennial Classics, HarperCollins, 1990.

———. *Zora Neale Hurston: Folklore, Memoirs, and Other Writings*. New York: Library of America, 1995.

Johnson, Barbara. "Metaphor, Metonymy and Voice in *Their Eyes Were Watching God*." *Black Literature and Literary Theory*. Edited by Henry Louis Gates, Jr. New York: Methuen, 1984.

Jordan, Jennifer. "Feminist Fantasies: Zora Neale Hurston's *Their Eyes Were Watching God*." *Tulsa Studies in Women's Literature* 7 (Spring 1988).

Lamothe, Daphne. "Vodou Imagery, African American Tradition, and Cultured Transformation in Zora Neale Hurston's *Their Eyes Were Watching God*." *Callaloo* 22, no. 1 (1999): 157-75.

Lillios, Anna. "'The Monstropolous Beast': The Hurricane in Zora Neale Hurston's *Their Eyes Were Watching God*." *The Southern Quarterly* 36, no. 3 (Spring 1998): 89-93.

Lowe, John. *Jump at the Sun: Zora Neale Hurston's Cosmic Comedy*. Urbana: University of Illinois Press, 1994.

Meisenhelder, Susan Edwards. *Hitting a Straight Lick with a Crooked Stick: Race and Gender in the Work of Zora Neale Hurston*. Tuscaloosa and London: University of Alabama Press, 1999.

Metraux, Alfred. *Voodoo in Haiti*. Trans. Hugo Charteris. New York: Schocken, 1972.

Mikell, Gwendolyn. "Feminism and Black Culture in the Ethnography of Zora Neale Hurston." *African-American Pioneers in Anthropology*. Edited by Ira E. Harrison and Faye V. Harrison. Urbana and Chicago: University of Illinois Press, 1999. 51-69.

Owusu, Heike. *Voodoo Rituals: A User's Guide*. New York: Sterling, 2002.

Pastras, Phil. *Dead Man Blues: Jelly Roll Morton Way Out West*. Berkeley and Los Angeles: University of California Press, 2001.

Pavlic, Edward M. "Papa Legba, Ouvrier Barriere Por Moi' Esu in *Their Eyes* and Zora Neale Hurston's Diasporic Modernism." *African American Review* 39, no. 1 (2005): 61-85.

Pinckney, Josephine. "A Pungent, Poetic Novel about Negroes [Review of *Jonah's Gourd Vine*]." New York Herald Tribune Books (6 May 1934): 7. Rpt. *Critical Essays on Zora Neale Hurston*. Edited by Gloria L. Cronin. New York: G. K. Hall, 1998. 33-34.

Plant, Deborah G. *Zora Neale Hurston: A Biography of the Spirit*. Westport: Praeger, 2007.

The Skeleton Key. Dir. Iain Softley. Perf. Kate Hudson, Gena Rowlands, John Hurt, Joy Bryant, Maxine Barnett, and Bill H. McKenzie. Universal Pictures, 2005. DVD. 104 minutes. Color. Languages: English, Español, Français. Dolby digital 5.1.

Southerland, Ellease. "The Influence of Voodoo on the Fiction of Zora Neale Hurston." In *Sturdy Black Bridges: Visions of Black Women in Literature*. Edited by Roseann P. Bell, Bettye J. Parker, and Beverly Guy-Sheftall. Garden City, NY: Anchor, 1979. 172-83.

Walker, Alice. "Looking for Zora." 1975. *The Best American Essays of the Century*. Edited by Joyce Carol Oates and Robert Atwan. Boston: Houghton Mifflin, 2000. 395-411.

———. "Zora Neale Hurston: A Cautionary Tale and A Partisan View." Foreword. *Zora Neale Hurston: A Literary Biography*. By Robert Hemenway. Urbana: University of Illinois Press, 1977. Rpt. *In Search of Our Mothers' Gardens: Womanist Prose*. San Diego, New York, London: Harcourt Brace, 1983. 83-92.

"West Africa: History." *Wikipedia*. October 14, 2007. En.wikipedia.org/wiki/West Africa.

Wheatley, Phillis. *Poems on Various Subjects, Religious and Moral*. London 1773. Rpt. Philadelphia: Joseph Crukshank, 1789. Microform.

———. *Poems on Various Subjects, Religious and Moral. The Norton Anthology of African American Literature*. Edited by Henry Louis Gates, Jr. and Nellie Y. McKay. New York: W. W. Norton & Company, 1996. 167-78.

"Zora Neale Hurston." *The Norton Anthology of African American Literature*. Edited by Henry Louis Gates, Jr., and Nellie Y. McKay. New York and London: W. W. Norton, 1997. 996-1065.

Chapter Three

Black African Spectral Dynamics in Contemporary Mexican Fiction

Shakespeare's Hamlet *Revisited*

In México nobody ever dies, or better, never do we say that the dead have
died.
-Juan Rulfo, *Cuadernos*

For in that sleep of death what dreams may come
When we have shuffled off this mortal coil
-William Shakespeare, *Hamlet*

Mexico shares with the rest of Latin America a variegated cultural history
marked by indigenous empires vying for predominance and Iberian empires
commissioning transatlantic voyages of discovery from 1415 until 1578.
Náhual ("spirit being") Indians enjoy a rich cultural heritage that converged
with Mexica (pronounced Meh-sheeh-kah) warrior creeds privileging priests
as mediums speaking for gods during possession rituals. Repelled by central
valley Náhual Indians in A.D. 1111, northern Mexica (European "Aztec")
Chichimecas[1] settled Culhuacán on Lake Texcoco, earned upward mobility
through military efficiency, and intermarried with Náhual Indian royalty to
form the Aztec Empire, 1427-1521 (Menchaca 34-35). Mexico's colonization relied on Spanish slave ships that imported 200,000 West African Vodun
("spirit") worshippers from 1519 until 1531. This chapter examines postcolonial implications of Vodun-Náhual-Mexica specters in contemporary Mexican fiction where Afro-Latino specters memorialize Mexico's Independence
Day, September 16, 1810, after centuries of occupation as "New Spain."[2]
While Mexico is ninety percent Roman Catholic, my critical analysis ex-

plores Mexican fiction's retention of religious belief in specters held by Black Vodunists and Náhuatl-speaking Mexica Indians. Mexican fiction initially mimicked the Spanish picaresque but shifted sharply to an Afrolatinidad perspective. In contrast to denunciation of specters in the first Mexican novel, *The Mangy Parrot* (*El Periquillo Sarniento*, 1816; rev. ed. 1842), by José Joaquin Fernández de Lizardi (b. Mexico City, 1776; d. 1827), spectral dynamics in fiction by Juan Rulfo (b. Jalisco, 1918, d. 1986), Hernán Lara Zavala (b. Mexico City, 1946), Álvaro Enrigue (b. Jalisco, 1969), and María Isabel Aguirre (b. Mexico City) navigate a timeline that reflects Mexico's heritage of Black African[3] and Náhual-Mexica belief in collaboration between the living and the sanctified spirits of the dead. Juan Rulfo, in "Manuscritos sobre los indios" (1995), laments the political, cultural, socioeconomic, and religious repercussions attendant upon the Aztec Empire's overthrow in 1521 by Castilian conquistador Hernán Cortés (b. Medellin, Spain, 1485; d. 1587) under Holy Roman Emperor Charles V and praises Indian cosmology, myths, and reverence for deities (*Cuadernos* 161-64). Lizardi revered Miguel de Cervantes (1547-1616) as Spain's consummate satirist (Vogeley 72-79). J. B. Priestley has observed, "Probably only Shakespeare has captured and delighted more minds than Cervantes. And by the strangest chance, they died on the same day, the 23rd of April 1616" (qtd. in Starkie's epigraph 15). Rulfo follows Shakespeare's *Hamlet, Prince of Denmark*, advancing Prince Hamlet's "To die, to sleep—To sleep, perchance to dream" (Act 3, scene 2, lines 64-65) in defining the novel as "a world where dream sometimes gets confused with life" (*Cuadernos* 169; my trans.). Examining *Pedro Páramo* in light of *Hamlet* emphasizes Rulfo's achievement while shining new light on post-colonialist ghost-portrayal in *Hamlet*.[3] Shakespeare's ghost-play crisscrosses lustful Claudius's and defiant Fortinbras's sacrilegious violations of King Hamlet's rights, mirroring the Danish-Norwegian Empire's infighting over colonized Poland. Across-the-board alignment with *Hamlet* accentuates *Pedro Páramo*'s postcolonial echoes in contemporary Mexican intertexts fêting Afro-Latino specters.

Postcolonial theorist Leela Gandhi observes that "mimicry" is a "slogan of postcolonial literary analysis" which studies the "paradigmatic moment of anti-colonial counter-textuality" (150). Lizardi's *The Mangy Parrot*, which is a protracted deathbed confession in which suspicion of ghosts differs from state-of-the-art renderings of specters in contemporary Mexican fiction, celebrates decolonization by using vernacular speech. Lizardi, a wealthy, well-read *Criollo* (Mexican-born Spaniard), was the son of a physician and a bookseller's daughter. Lizardi's novel appeared during the Mexican War of Independence, 1810-1821, when combined *Criollo,* mestizo (European and Amerindian), mulatto (Spanish and Black), and zambo (Amerindian and Black) guerilla armies fought Spanish rule. Nevertheless, Lizardi emulates Iberian literature, disdaining ghosts as aberrant, devious, and substandard phenomena. *The Mangy Parrot*'s protagonist Don Pedro, while he lies on his deathbed, wants his confessor, Father Pelayo, to stay at his bedside until he is dead even though, he boasts, he is not "'afraid of the devils, visions, or ghosts that they say appear to the dying'" and believes that it is "a vulgar superstition to think that everyone who dies sees those specters, because God doesn't need to use such ethereal puppets to punish or terrorize a sinner. The sinner's own bad conscience, and the remorse it brings at this hour, are the only demons and bogeymen his soul can see, confounded by the memory of his bad life, his lack of repentance, and his servile dread of an exasperated and righteous god; all the rest are the gullible notions of the foolish mob" (530-31). In contradistinction to spectral robustness in contemporary Mexican fiction, Pedro's epitaph attributes spectral haunting to a decedent's sinfulness, and not to specters' righteousness: "Here lies Pedro Sarmiento / Commonly known as Periquillo Sarniento. / In life he was but a sinner: / Nothing in his death. Passerby, / Whoever you be, / Pray that God grant him / Eternal rest" (535).

While Lizardi mimics Cervantes's epic novel *Don Quixote* (1587), Juan Rulfo is a postcolonial author who defends the human rights of indigenous natives whose lexicon has been obscured by centuries of foreign occupation.[4] Rulfo's postcolonial ethos is almost eclipsed by the stunningly innovative narrative techniques that make *Pedro Páramo* (1955) an outstanding twentieth-century novel. Although Rulfo read Lizardi's novel (*Cuadernos* 176), scholars favorably compare *Pedro Páramo*'s style to William Faulkner, Henry James, and Franz Kafka, extoling Rulfo's narrative artistry. But scant attention is paid to connecting style and content, none to assessing Rulfo's role as a postcolonial novelist and adherent of Afrolatinidad.

Pedro Páramo's contribution to Mexican literary tradition has a comprehensive critical context; indeed, Rulfo shares with poet-playwright William Shakespeare (baptized April 26, 1564) a capacity to espouse belief in Vodun specters in a Latin-derived *chef-d'oeuvre*. Shakespeare and Rulfo portray specters in ways that indicate familiarity with time-honored West African Vodun theological beliefs. While Rulfo portrays ghosts to countermand imperial Spain's colonization of Mexico, Shakespeare depicts a ghost purposefully striving to restore ethical and moral order in the Danish Empire (1536-1953). Occasioned by the British Empire's inception when King James I (b. Edinburgh Castle, 1566; d. Herefordshire, 1625) consolidated England, Scotland, Ireland, and Wales in 1603, Shakespeare's *Hamlet* (2003; performed 1600-1601; published 1604) closely follows the plot and characters portrayed in an early thirteenth-century Hamlet story that was written, in Latin,[5] by Saxo Grammaticus (ca. 1150-1216), an ecclesiastic who compiled *Historia* (or *Gesta*) *Danica*, "Stories / Deeds of the Danes" (Raffel 2003, xv), about "a prince, Amletha, whose father, the king of Denmark, was murdered by his brother, Fengo, [who then] married his brother's widow, Gerutha. . . . Fengo ships Amletha off to England [where he eventually marries the English king's daughter, returns to Denmark, kills Fengo, and takes the throne]" (xv-xvi). *Hamlet* portrays Danish usurper Claudius undoing his brother King Hamlet's trouncing an uprising of ethnic Norwegian inhabitants of Poland.

Both Shakespeare and Rulfo fashion interpenetrating sociopolitical stories. Counterpointing Claudius's sexual lust for Queen Gertrude and political lust for the Danish throne, Shakespeare portrays King Hamlet's ghost as an advocate for justice, urging Prince Hamlet to take corrective action against Claudius's incestuous passion and lawless usurpation of the throne. Claudius short-circuits *Hamlet*'s two stories. Obsessed by adulterous love for Gertrude, who is his sister-in-law, Claudius scarcely notices courtier Polonius's death and remains oblivious to the advance of Norway's militia. Rulfo, like Shakespeare, shows how political decline and fall are inextricably bound up with ethical malfeasance and moral decadence. Rulfo modifies Shakespeare's focus on royal households, taking a grassroots approach to depict a socially-stratified community. Pedro Páramo is a local political boss or *cacique*. The origin of the term *cacique*'s provenance is the "plural family" practice in the "West African culture of Dahomey" where two or more wives live in separate huts with their children. Each wife spends "a native week of four days with the common husband, cooking his food, washing his cloths, sleeping in his house, and then making way for the next. Her children remain in their mother's hut. With pregnancy, she drops out of this routine, and ideally, in the interest of her child's health and her own, does not again visit her husband until the child has been born and weaned. This means a period of from three to four years, since infants are nursed two years or longer" (Herskovits 64, 47). Pedro Páramo weds Juan Preciado's mother, Dolores, against her will only because she holds legal ownership of *Media Luna*. Páramo lusts after Susana San Juan, who remains faithful to her high-spirited husband Florencio, killed in battle. Both Shakespeare and Rulfo portray specters in a positive light as deceased victims emblematizing a spiritual force plying legal and moral opposition to corruption in the world of political affairs and sexual politics.

Avoiding the idea that ghosts haunt wrongdoers, Shakespeare and Rulfo depict phantoms from the past, commingling theologies rooted in Vodun religious beliefs disseminated during Europe's renaissance, when African slaves' transatlantic transport enabled the Portuguese Empire, Spanish Empire, and English Empire to colonize the Americas during the Middle Passage, 1500-1900. Obliquely impugning colonialism, Shakespeare's *Hamlet* and Rulfo's *Pedro Páramo* concatenate spectral dynamics, accounting for family tragedies where ghosts emblematize imperialism's devastation. Claudius treacherously kills his brother King Hamlet. Similarly, Páramo's son Miguel murders Rentería's brother (26). Rentería, who blesses Susana's fidelity to Florencio, resembles Horatio, a Christian who bolsters Prince Hamlet's faith in an invisible spirit clothed in "cómplete steel" that emblematizes Ogun, Vodun god of iron and war (Act 1, scene 4, line 52). Officiously, Claudius retaliates against Prince Hamlet's elimination of conniving courtier Polonius by delegating sycophants Rosencrantz and Guildenstern to abduct and assassinate Prince Hamlet. Similarly, Pedro Páramo responds to Don Fulgar Sedano's death at the hands of revolutionaries, peremptorily sending for "boa constrictor" El Tilcuate then resuming his lovesick mooning over Susana, who, like Queen Gertrude, is haunted by wifely memories of passionate lovemaking while smothered-to-death by a possessive, lovesick despot. As Claudius never sees King Hamlet's ghost, so, too, Pedro Páramo is alienated from Susana: "But what world was Susana San Juan living in? That was one of the things Pedro Páramo would never know" (93). In a grief-stricken, tormented rage, Abundio Martínez stabs Pedro Páramo, whose cruelty transforms him into a rock pile, a monument to the dehumanization he perpetrated.

Although *Hamlet*'s plot and story have provenance in a medieval Danish Catholic saga written in Latin, King Hamlet's ghost is an artistic adaptation of Vodun belief in reincarnated spirits and Christian faith in the Holy Ghost, or Holy Spirit. *Hamlet* juxtaposes Vodun and Christian views of specters. Shakespeare wrote *Othello, The Moor*[6] *of Venice* in 1603, and *Hamlet* unveils knowledge of African Vodun theological belief in spirits of two kinds: Prince Hamlet's response to King Hamlet's ghost suggests Vodun belief in sanctified ancestral spirits while his university classmate Horatio's learned discourse links King Hamlet's ghost to usurper Claudius, suggesting zombie, or soulless body, imagery. While Horatio sees the apparition as a zombie-like sign of evil, Prince Hamlet respects the "honest ghost" as a virtuous and creditable messenger spirit (Act 1, scene 5, line 138). Prince Hamlet regards the apparition as a hallowed spirit and trusts its allegations that Claudius committed regicide and incestuous adultery. Scholarly Horatio asserts his Christianity: "Before my God, / I might not this belief / Without the sensible and true avouch / Of mine own eyes," he avows (Act 1, scene 1, lines 56-58). Horatio deems the ghost to be an intelligible portent of evil; "This bodes some strange eruption to our state," he asserts (Act 1, scene 1, line 69). Horatio deduces that Danish king Hamlet's recent victory over Norwegian king Fortinbras is undermined now that Claudius is king. He likens Denmark's statutory occupation of colonial territories to a short-lived Roman victory. Cognizant of ironic innuendo in Claudius's allegation that King Hamlet was stung by a serpent—Christian symbol of evil—Horatio recalls that legions of spirits clothed in white—Vodun color symbolizing death (and life)—heralded the fall of the Holy Roman Empire, which extended from Britain to North Africa. Horatio declares, "The graves stood tenantless and the sheeted dead / Did squeak and gibber in the Roman streets" (Act 1, scene 1, lines 115-16). Showing keen understanding of Vodun moral theology,

Horatio states that at dawn the ghost "started like a guilty thing," then the "extravagant and erring spirit hies / to his confine" (Act 1, scene 1, lines 154-55). According to Vodun doctrine, supreme divinity Olódúmarè allows ghosts to appear only at night, constrained to return to their graves before daybreak. Prince Hamlet subscribes to the divine right of kings doctrine. He esteems the ghost as a visible sign of divine grace conferred on kingship, yet he is struck by wonderment. "King, father, royal Dane. O, answer me! / Let me not burst in ignorance, but tell / Why thy canonized bones, hearsed in death, / Have burst their cerements, why the sepulcher / Wherein we saw thee quietly inurned / Hath oped his ponderous and marble jaws, / To cast thee up again" (Act 1, scene 4, lines 45-51). Horatio tells Prince Hamlet that the ghost "might . . . draw you into madness" (Act 1, scene 4, lines 73-74). Horatio's warning that Prince Hamlet will be possessed by a funky zombie-spirit prompts Prince Hamlet to "put an antic disposition on" at the end of Act 1 (Act 1, scene 5, line 172).

Consistent with King Hamlet's divine right to bestow privileged knowledge, the ghost summons Prince Hamlet to a private audience. Only Prince Hamlet hears his "father's spirit" (Act 1, scene 5, line 9) demand that he "Revenge his foul and most unnatural murder" (Act 1, scene 5, lines 25). Consistent with Vodun theological authority deeming death as a crossroads demarcating a separation of the living from the dead, Prince Hamlet recognizes that the apparition is the spirit separated from the flesh of King Hamlet, which the ghost's discourse demonstrates in authorizing Prince Hamlet to avenge "his"—not "my"— "unnatural murder." Shakespeare accounts for Prince Hamlet's academic ally Horatio's erudite opinion in the play's plot-line when the ghost tells Prince Hamlet that Claudius poured poison into his brother King Hamlet's ear and committed "damnèd incest" on the "royal bed of Denmark" (Act 1, scene 5, lines 82-83). When Prince Hamlet swears "by Saint Patrick," the canonized Roman Catholic who led snakes overrunning Ireland into the ocean, *Hamlet* invokes Vodun divinity Damballah, a deity usually worshipped or envisioned more generally as the snake-like supreme creation god. An avatar of Damballah, Moses parted the Red Sea with his snake-like staff to free enslaved Hebrews. On the other hand, Claudius incarnates the Biblical evil serpent because he violates Mosaic Law forbidding marriage of a man to his brother's widow. It is significant that the ghost commands Horatio and Marcellus to "Swear by his sword" that they will not reveal the ghost's presence among them because this oath ritual forwards a sacred aboriginal African rite (Act 1, scene 5, line 161). The ghost exudes its occult origins as a primordial entity emanating from Pre-Christian Vodun theological dogmata.

Critical commentaries on Rulfo's readings of Scandinavian authors corroborate my discovery of parallels between Shakespeare's *Hamlet, Prince of Denmark* and Rulfo.[7] Biographical facts support intriguing similarities not hitherto observed, salient parallels that could not have failed to register in Rulfo's mind. Rulfo, like Prince Hamlet, was deprived of his birthright by violence. Rulfo was born in Apulco, in the Pacific coast state Jalisco, but "his family lost its *parcelas* of land in the armed struggles during the Mexican revolution, 1910-1920, and the Cristero revolt" against the anti-Catholic Mexican government, 1926-1929 (Stavans xi). Similar to Prince Hamlet, Rulfo lost his father, who was killed when he was six, and four years later, "his mother had a heart attack and died" (Stavans xii). Shakespeare's portrayal of Denmark in *Hamlet*—Marcellus observes that "There is something rotten in the state of Denmark" (Act 1, scene 4, line 90) —parallels Rulfo's portrayal of Comala in *Pedro Páramo*. Rulfo "often talked about the decay in the towns where he grew up and about how "the government had forgotten its inhabitants" (Stavans xii). While Prince Hamlet left Elsinore to attend Wittenburg University in Lutherstadt, Saxony (est. 1502 by Friedrich III), Rulfo left Jalisco to attend Academia Militar Nacional and then to study literature and law at Universidad Nacional Autónoma de México in Mexico City. Prince Hamlet's interest in the ghost is whetted by castle celebrants "swagg'ring up-spring reels" to "kettle-drum" beats and the "bray" of a "trumpet" in rites similar to Vodun dance rituals (Act 1, scene 4, lines 9-11). Rulfo's attribution of authority to specters arose when he researched aboriginal traditions, solidifying his ethnic concerns.

Pedro Páramo establishes a distinctive pattern integrating Shakespearean motifs and Vodun-Náhual-Mexica spectral representations. Pedro Páramo's spurious downplaying of the "Rumor" that Miguel Páramo murdered Rentería's brother and "raped" his daughter Ana (26) is an ironic self-parody that mirrors *Hamlet*'s play-within-the-play "The Murder of Gonzago" wherein a costumed actor mimics Claudius's murder of King Hamlet (Act 2, scene 2, line 521). Rulfo's psychological realism conjoins Náhual and Catholic religiosity. One Sunday, a "fine rain" brings Pacific coast Apango (Náhual-Coixcas) Indians with their "rosaries" of chamomile, rosemary, and thyme, to sell herbs in Comala (86). They "pray to the Virgin" at the Catholic Church, while Náhual rain god Tlaloc empowers a specter to talk to Susana. Tlaloc presides over Susana remembering her father Bartolomé (before he was killed in Andromeda coal mine) lower his little daughter underneath floorboards where she saw by lamplight only skulls instead of "gold coins"— post-colonialist imagery evoking natives' martyrdom to imperial greed for gold (91). Susana's father's name honors Father Bartolomé de las Casas (1484-1566), who defended Indians as "rational beings with souls" (Menchaca 52). Presently, Susana glimpses a "shadowy figure on the ceiling, its head looming above her face," saying, "'I am your father'" (92). In a polychromatic atmosphere of masculine fire (candle-flame) and air (wind), Catholic Father Rentería opens the door holding a candle, casting the black shadow, a Vodun-derived ghost-figure, of her Náhual father Bartolomé's

soul "come to tell [Susana] that 'Florencio is dead,'" which she already
knows because imbued with her husband Florencio's Náhual-Mexica life-
force (93).

Pedro Páramo's spectral dynamics transform Comala's death-spiral into
a fluctuating whirlpool of ghostly voices. Although Preciado promised his
dying mother to obtain her bequest from his father Pedro Páramo, Abundio is
his guardian spirit in Comala. Initially, Abundio, like King Hamlet's ghost,
arises from the past, whereas Preciado, like Prince Hamlet a flesh-and-blood
protagonist, occupies the present. Abundio announces that Páramo is dead
and that Páramo was his father, too. As the novel progresses, past and present
switch places. After Preciado dies, his consciousness envelops Comala, his
mind maneuvering like a camera-eye, recording scenes that interconnect past
and present. Time is multidimensional so that Preciado witnesses his half-
brother Abundio commit parricide. Páramo's death occurred in the past, yet
Abundio's slaying of Páramo is the novel's final action.

Pedro Páramo epitomizes Rulfo's observation "For the Aztecs and all of
the Mesoamerican pueblos, the basis of life and actions was fundamentally
religious" especially after "Franciscan friars built convents and cathedrals
where nuns initiated the spiritual conquest of New Spain" (*Cuadernos* 165,
my trans.). Anthroponomastics reinforce Rulfo's religious life-in-death motifs. The anthroponym "Pedro [Peter] Páramo" suggests Apostle Peter (Latin
petra means "rock") to whom Christ said "Thou art Peter, and upon this rock,
I will build my church" (Matthew 16:18). This subtextual allusion counter-
weights libertine Pedro Páramo licentiously propagating life while simultaneously destroying it; indeed, his children are doomed at birth. The patronym
"Pár-amo" implies deception and deceit: In the guise of love (Spanish *amo*
denotes "I love"), Pára-mo, zombie-like, consumes the town "through"
(Spanish *para*) disseminating disease and death (*morir* denotes "to die").
Comala comprises doomed children of women who incestuously generated a
population debilitated by birth defects and curtailed lives.[8] Spectral imagery
defines "Co-mala" (*con mal* means "with evil") as a town plagued by agoniz-
ing illnesses, a rock-strewn graveyard. Abundio's ghost motivates Juan Preciado, an epitome of urbane Náhual townspeople, to assimilate colonized
Comala's oppression. Aptly, Abundio—descendant of elite Tolmec-Mexica
warrior clans that defended the Náhual Indians, built the Aztec Empire, and
opposed Montezuma's hospitality to Cortés—slays *cacique*[9] Pedro Páramo.

Counterpointing Vodun cosmological elevation of storm gods, *Pedro
Páramo* juxtaposes poetic imagery of Náhual-Mexica nature divinities. Sun
god Huitzilopochtli, "virginally conceived child of ancient earth goddess
Coatlicue (literally, 'serpent skirt')," at noon was "carried into the middle of
the sky by the spirits of warriors who had died in battle, or on the sacrificial
stone" and at sunset "the ghosts of women who had died in childbirth re-
turned him to earth" (Thomas 11-12). Similar to Vodun *loa* (earth and water

deity) Damballah and *orisha* (heavenly divinity) Olódúmarè (God Almighty), Huitzilopochtli was a chieftain who was deified after his death. This tradition originated during 600 B.C.–1700 A.D. with Yoruba, Ibo, and Fon in Nigeria, Benin, and Togo, venerating Vodun thunder-and-lightning god Shango. While Náhual Indians favored Coatlicue and Tlaloc, Mexica warriors exalted Huitzilopochtli, whose prestige as central deity burgeoned along with the Aztec Empire. Rulfo invokes Huitzilopochtli's presence when Juan Preciado sees "shimmering sunlight" powerfully transforming the plain into a "transparent lake" (5). At dusk, "little village children" play, their shadows illuminated by "pale yellow sunlight" (7). Náhual-Mexica elders viewed children as closest to the gods, comparing a beautiful child to "a precious feather" or "precious stone bracelet" (Thomas 21). Gold symbolizes Huitzilopochtli's sanctifying presence. Náhual-Mexica "sanctuaries" were guarded by "belts of snakes made of gold" and "necklaces of human heads, also in gold" (Thomas 300). Huitzilopochtli's resilience fosters moonlit memories. At nightfall, Juan Preciado hears his mother's voice saying "You will hear the voice of my memories stronger than the voice of my death" (8).

Childhood memories augment Pedro Páramo's status as a military commander and prolific progenitor. Pedro Páramo looms as a vibrant polytheistic emblem. Evocative images of Pedro Páramo as a small boy in a "privy" hearing rainwater drip "Plink! Plink!" from roof tiles while daydreaming about "Susana" are phallocentric (11-12). Traditional icons of Ghede, Vodun guardian of the dead, are the phallus, tomb, and cross. Pedro Páramo does not pray as his Catholic grandmother wants; instead, he "just [watches] it rain" (13). Vehemently, he hunts for Susana, whom he sees as a ghost-girl hiding "in God's immensity." Huizilopochtli's name means "Hummingbird on the left" or "of the south" (Thomas 11), and little Pedro Páramo hears "whirring" hummingbirds' wings when he seizes twenty of twenty-four centavos at Sacred Heart Shrine (14). Thomas remarks that Huitzilopochtli, Tlaloc, Quetzalcoatl, and "the capricious Tezcatlipoca" were "the real rulers of the Mexica" (13). Huitzilopochtli reigns over daytime's sun-drenched plain and nighttime's incessant rain. Vodun storm god Shango counterpoints Náhual-Mexica rain god Tlaloc's "quiet drizzle" of "weeping "raindrops" with "lightning flashes," coupled with Shango's wife Oya's wind-bursts, turning young Pedro Páramo's attention to Catholic Indian women praying for "forgiveness of sins and the resurrection of the body" (15). Pedro Páramo's mother, a Virgin Mary / Coatlicue apparition, chastises the boy for not saying his "'Rosary'" (15). Although he is a devout Catholic woman's son, Pedro Páramo embodies the unpredictability of Vodun *loa* Legba, a trickster god at life's crossroads, and capriciousness of "mischievous" Mexica deity Tezcatlipoca, an "arbitrary god" who "stood for total power," causing "confusion on earth" as a "master of disguise" (Thomas 185-86). Yet, filial redemption is evoked when the boy obeys his mother by taking only a peso from her flowerpot, spontaneously leaving twenty centavos as a result of her nurturing efforts. Pedro Páramo's mother is an archetypal Holy Mother standing at a spiritual threshold illuminated by her candle. Her dark "shadow stretched toward the ceiling" symbolizes Vodun divinity Oshun, Mother of Africa. Flickering firelight on the "roof beams" replicate her shadow "in fragments," reminiscent of a Mexica mosaic (Greek *mousa* or "muse") frieze (15). Her "sobbing" mingles with the "rain," while the "church clock" tolls "hour after hour" of "telescoped" time, evoking Pedro Páramo's salvation by the intercession of "Our Lady of Sorrow," invoked as a matriarchal specter's visitation.

The title of Juan Rulfo's *The Burning Plain* (2008; *El llano en llamas*, 1953) pays homage to Huitzilopochtli. Several stories complement *Hamlet*-inspired Christian and Vodun-Náhual-Mexica motifs in *Pedro Páramo*. Rulfo's supernatural fables almost imperceptibly render spectral consciousness, compressing plots and evoking multiethnic politico-religious beliefs. Exquisitely, "The Man" ("El Hombre") reprises *Hamlet*'s pursuit-plot, depicting traditional Mexican cultural values and elaborating Christian and Vodun concepts of God's grace. "Paso del Norte" comprises spectral exaltation of *Hamlet*'s father-son bond. Rulfo, in "Remember" (Acuerdate"), pays tribute to his predecessor Lizardi as father of the Mexican novel, portraying ghosts as conscience figures haunting malefactors. Rulfo invokes memory's power to bridge life and death, the visible and the invisible.

In "The Man," Rulfo creates a cosmologically intricate narrative design that alternates between two men, José Alcancia and Urquidi, then two viewpoints, sheepherder and sheriff. Urquidi's ghost pursues José, who shot Urquidi because he slew José's brother. A repentant Catholic, José regrets killing not just one man, but Urquidi's entire family. Significantly, José, a Joseph avatar, did not slay Urquidi's interred newborn, a Vodun-derived rebirth symbol. Urquidi anticipates each repositioning in José's endeavor to cross the river. For this reason, Urquidi is certain he will attain his objective of capturing his foe. Remorsefully, José abandons his machete, a Vodun-derived symbol that shines like a "lifeless snake"; he renounces Ogun to admire Damballah's "river," which "winds like a serpent coiled on the green earth" (35). Sighting a flock of chachalacas symbolizing the Urquidi family's souls, he crosses himself three times, praying for them to "Forgive me" (35). Meantime, the sunless sky reminds Urquidi of the Sunday José disrupted burial rites for his newborn baby. Huitzilopochtli's absence impacted José, who, unable to discern his target, blindly killed everybody. Paradoxically, Huizilopochtli's intervention vouchsafes José's family against retributive retaliation.

The fable's second half foregrounds a sheepherder watching José from a superior vantage-point atop an embankment, where spiritual awareness intersects with the material body. Momentously, José, exhausted, reaches the summit, where he eats tortillas and drinks ewe's milk with the sheepherder, commemorating Christ's Last Supper. José's contrition bridges a cultural lacuna. Urquidi's blood oaths vengefully to kill José's brother and then José contrast sharply to José's decimating the Urquidis goaded by fear for the security of his family. Urquidi accomplishes his goal of shooting José in the back of his neck. As Prince Hamlet kills Claudius in execution of the ghost's command, Sheriff Licenciado fulfills Urquidi's ghost's mission to avenge the Urquidi family. The sheepherder finds José floating face-down in the river. Voluntarily, he contacts Lucenciado, a bulwark of Spain's colonial infra-structure who accuses him of aiding and abetting José during his attempts to flee the arm of the law. He protests, "All he did was ask me for something to eat and talk to me about [his wife] and children, with tears running down his face" (42). Overwhelmed by Lucienciado's interrogation tactics, the sheep-herder renounces his charitable treatment of José, as when Apostle Peter, intimidated by Roman soldiers, denied knowing Christ. Crucially, José lives via the good sheepherder's narrative. The sheepherder's account of José as "a dead man in a pool of the river" blends Catholic and Vodun spiritual rebirth imagery. José is a vigilante who defends his family. The sheepherder re-sponds compassionately to José, who avenged his brother's murder, then repents, and cleanses his spirit. By Christian and Vodun-Náhual-Mexica standards, José, baptized, is shriven of sin. Likewise, Ghede, Vodun god of the afterlife, enables Urquidi's ghost to punish the Urquidi family's slayer.

Juan Rulfo's "Paso del Norte" is a ghost tale about a Polonius-like widower and his Laertes-like *paisano* son, whose Ophelia-like sister died. An opening dialogue establishes life-death symbiosis in a son who respects his father's wisdom, expressed in maxims like "If the bell doesn't ring, it's because there's no clapper" (122), which parodies Polonius's advice "Give thy thoughts no tongue / Nor any unproportioned thought his act" (1.3.59-60). Rulfo's tale illustrates Laertes's defense of Polonius's farewell speeches: "A double blessing is a double grace: Occasion smiles upon a second leave" (Act 1, scene 3, lines 53-54). Laertes's leave-takings to France parallel the *paisano*'s migrant-worker lifestyle. The poverty-stricken patri-arch, a fireworks concession stand proprietor, calls himself "a dead man," an epithet confirmed by the fact that he knows about his son's wedding but not his five grandchildren (125). The *paisano* tells his father's ghost his family is starving-to-death and he must head to Oregon with co-worker Estanislado to pick apples or lay railroad track. Later, the son returns home as a specter after border patrol riflemen fire fatal volleys: "Father, they killed us. They pep-pered us with bullets until they killed all of us" (127). A Fortinbras-like "immigration officer" wrongfully blames the "lights" and "firing" on "the Apaches" (129). Despite his "uniform" and "big pistol," he denies army affiliation when the *paisano* addresses him respectfully as "sergeant" (128). Subtly and artistically, Rulfo's Mexican ghost yarn evokes Ghede's power in

Prince Hamlet's dying observation, "this fell [fierce, ruthless] sergeant, death, / Is strict in his arrest [of time]" (Act 5, scene 2, lines 322-23; interpolations in source). As Shakespeare depicts Afro-Latin theology, so, too, Rulfo validates the Vodun-Náhual-Mexica spectral ethos. The border skirmish allocates legal limits, but also differing religious beliefs about the meaning of life (and death).

Rulfo uses startling key-word allusions to *Hamlet.* In *Pedro Páramo,* Preciado tells Doña Edviges Dyada that Dolores Preciado left Comala to live in Colima with her sister, "my Aunt Gertrudis," he testifies (19). In "Remember". ("Acuérdate"), an allusive title that truncates the ghost's command to Prince Hamlet "Remember me," the imperative mood prevails (46). The Marcellus-like narrator tells his Horatio-like interlocutor to remember nobleman Don Urbano's son, Gómez. Classmates reminisce over the antics of prankster Gómez, whom his uncle Fidencio punitively beat until "he got so mad he left the village," later returning as "a policeman" whose "hate" showed in "his gun" and refusal to speak to, greet, or recognize anybody (114). Gómez, Hamlet-like, kills his Laertes-like brother-in-law and is arrested. He secures a "tree of his choice" and ties a "rope around his [own] neck" (114) which burlesques Claudius stabbed with the poisoned rapier tip he intended for Prince Hamlet.

Hernán Lara Zavala's short story "Hammering Away" (2009) illustrates pre-colonial Vodun-Náhual-Mexica belief that death represents a two-way crossing-over; the body is buried yet the soul continues to have palpable life in a spirit-world bridged to the material world. Conceptually, death entails the soul's reversible passage from visible body to disembodied spirit. Hitting his father's gravestone with a hammer, Ogun's symbol, a drunken son bewails his life-in-death existence as a zombie decommissioned by his father's spirit. The cameo appearance of his cousin, a pilgrim, illustrates the death-in-life / life-in-death theological concept in a Vodun poem: "I came to drink with my friend, / and find him I could not. / O Death, who taketh away Life / And giveth no day at court,/ A day will come and I shall see him again. / Aye, I shall see him . . . / For I too am going toward death" (Dracher 61-62). In "Hammering Away," Zavala portrays the all-inclusive life of Antonio, whose deceased father devoted a lifetime to operating his neighborhood grocery store *The Embassy,* expanding it and offering customers merchandise, including "candles, rope, hats, stationery, little gifts, and some toys" (441). One day in the year 2005, Antonio disappears. He leaves the store to spend a day with his cousin, a writer who traveled from Mexico City to take Antonio to *The Queen Bee,* a local bar, then make a pilgrimage to their "grandparents' graves" (437). Establishing a sympathetic perspective, the first sentence asserts "Alvarito was very worried" (435). The second sentence starts interweaving strands of ambiguity and ambivalence that permeate the narrative, building accumulatively to a climactic open ending.

Zavala attenuates Rulfo's Shakespearean elements while retaining the notion of political conflict centering on patriarchal dominance where a son deals with a categorical imperative to obey his father's ghost. Rulfo expands *Hamlet*'s focus on royal families vying for geopolitical control, adapting imperialist infighting among noble aristocrats by employing spectral dynamics to depict a Mexican town's collective suffering at the hands of an overlord. Zavala portrays a petit bourgeois family in which the son carries his resentment against his father, especially oppressive after he dies, with him until his dying day, which he spends bitterly spewing his grievances at his dead father's sepulcher. While Rulfo replicates and multiplies the murderous and incestuous relationships in *Hamlet* that constitute the *raison d'être* of King Hamlet's ghost, Zavala evokes the felt presence and overriding power of a father through the cowed and angry perspective of a son driven by his overbearing father's will. Similarly to Prince Hamlet's relationship with King Hamlet's ghost, Zavala's protagonist son views his father as an evanescent, hence unconquerable, supernatural force that dominates his life. The son is stifled, buried beneath his dead father's influence, living as a stultified funky zombie.

Part I launches a bifurcated visible-invisible design. Interacting with Alvarito, an employee, and Chavéz, a creditor, Antonio mimics his father's authoritarianism. Alvarito is concerned about Antonio because that day, shortly before closing time, Mr. Chavéz, the town's loan shark, belligerently demanded payment of the three thousand pesos Antonio owes him. As the small business's conscientious bookkeeper, Alvarito feels a burden of responsibility to repay the loan on demand, but he was forced to make excuses because Antonio left explicit instructions not to dispense any money without his authorization. Alvarito's threefold worry hinges on financial considerations, alarm about Antonio's well-being, and misgivings over his boss's inexplicable absence. Zavala uses indirect discourse to delve into Alvarito's disquietude. Alvarito, filled with foreboding "set off to find out where the devil Antonio could be," aware that "He'd never been away for so long without any notice" (435).

Zitilchén is a tiny town that thrives thanks to the social network formed by members of the property-owning bourgeois merchants and their clientele. Alvarito is able to piece together a scenario that might reveal the whereabouts of his errant employer. When he ascertains from townsfolk that Antonio had drinks with his cousin at *The Queen Bee* at around three o'clock, Alvarito determines that they could not still be there because owner Samuel Cervera "always closes by six," Alvarito remembers (435). When Alvarito nears *The Queen Bee*, he sees it is indeed closed and proceeds to the Cervera residence. Alvarito apologizes for disturbing them, explaining, "I'm worried because of his diabetes and high blood pressure, and the doctor gave him strict orders not to drink" (437). Cervera attests to the intoxicated condition of Antonio when he left the bar. He tells Alvarito that Antonio grabbed a bottle of "that rotgut Holcatzin" in a drunken stupor and headed with his cousin to the churchyard.

Part II shifts from Alvarito's perspective to reveal Antonio "alone in the churchyard" in abject misery amidst the "sepulchral silence of the night" (437). Comprising the main body of the narrative, Part II confirms the bar owner's advisory to Alvarito in Part I. High-strung Antonio suffers medical problems despite his staid lifestyle, ailments exacerbated by sibling rivalry and longing to play heroic machismo roles bred by romantic imaginings. Inebriated, he addresses his dead father. He delivers his tirade emphatically, rhythmically tapping his father's gravestone with his father's hammer, which he keeps in his pocket so that "'I always have a little part of you with me,'" he ironizes (437). Although he inherited the store, sixty-five-year-old Antonio continues to be spurred, as he has all his life, by his allegiance to his father, who opened the grocery-store financed by a loan from Antonio's Uncle Leandro when Antonio was eight. Christmas 1948 brought gifts for his sister Conchita but none for Antonio. Antonio, who continually had to "hide out" in a "great big guayaba tree," because he angered his father, "never got a single present" (439). When Antonio was nine, he had his heart set on a "toy soldier wearing a gold helmet, sitting on a chestnut horse with a French[10] flag in his hand and a sword at his waist" (441). He excelled in history and geography so he was furious that his request letters and food offerings were untouched. Vengefully, he took the toy soldier from the display window "like a bolt of lightning" and put it under his hammock (441). But in the morning he discovered his father had put it back, "as if nothing had happened" (443). He rebuked Antonio for being "'crazy'" (445). Christmas-time is an intersection where Antonio, emblematizing indigenous Mexica and imperial Spain's militarism, suffers as a maverick in Zitilchén, an imaginary town symbolizing Náhual political and cultural values. Antonio's perennially thwarted desire and fanatical pleas to get a toy soldier for Christmas alienate his Náhual father. Antonio's father-son relationship is suspended scaffolding that paradigmatically represents historic hostilities—highly-literate Náhual townspeople against fearless Mexica warriors, native Indians against Spanish conquerors—subtly evoking a multidimensional postcolonial ethos. Antonio is haunted by his dead father's memory; furthermore, Antonio provoked his father as an epitomic emblem of global conquest. Christmas-time is a Vodun crossroads where Antonio is a spoiler—whether Mexica warrior or Spanish soldier—that alienates his Náhual-like father.

Zavala's artistic and philosophical rendering of Antonio's Hamlet-like declamation depicts Antonio as an imperialist specter in the eyes of his father, who sees Antonio as a politically-portentous threat to his personal freedom to honor Náhual family values. Defensively, he polarizes his detractor. Similarly to Cortés's siege of Tenochtitlan in 1520, Antonio's Náhual father blockades Antonio as his would-be imperial Mexica-Spanish conquistador son. Without battling Antonio, his father resists opposition using a logistics-based strategy. As Cortés deliberately weakened the Mexica warriors, cutting off their food and water supply, so, too, father discourages son through deprivation tactics. Cortés proselytized his troops at Tlaxcala temple, declaring that his spiritual purpose reaped "honour and commercial profit"; moreover, he "denounced the veneration of idols" (Thomas 455-56). Antonio is a martyr to Legba, divinity of life's crossroads, because his dead father, sponsored by Ghede, possesses Antonio, forcing him to inhabit the ground between life and death.

Both Hernán Lara Zavala's "Hammering Away" and Álvaro Enrigue's "On the Death of the Author" have been honored with publication in the Dalkey bilingual edition of *Best Contemporary Mexican Fiction* (2009). While Zavala's postcolonial concern in "Hammering Away" is nuanced, anecdotal, and emblematized in the son's frustrated ambition to receive a toy soldier as a Christmas gift, Álvaro Enrigue in "On the Death of the Author" foregrounds postcolonial themes by expanding the idea of systematized role reversal, which is a deeply embedded undercurrent in Shakespeare's *Hamlet* and Rulfo's *Pedro Páramo*. Enrigue explores historical boundary-shifts between Mexico and the United States. The Treaty of Guadalupe Hidalgo settled the Mexican-U.S. War, 1845-1846, stipulating that Mexico immediately withdraw from California, New Mexico, Arizona, Nevada, Utah and parts of Wyoming and Colorado. Enrigue's "On the Death of the Author" has a compellingly impassioned tone stemming from the choice of the narrator, a professor, to write a profoundly personal narrative. Moreover, the short story conveys autobiographical immediacy, as suggested in the epigraph that Enrigue uses to set the mood for the professor's story. Enrique's epigraph is a couplet excerpted from Renaissance Iberian poet Garcilaso de la Vega (1503-1536): "Written upon my soul is your expression / And everything I want to write about you" (33).

Poignantly the narrating professor is haunted to his soul's depths by Ishi's life-and-death existence. Subtly, the story insinuates the epic past glory of the Wild West Indian nations and the vast sweep of their empires in North, Central, and South America. Evoking indigenous nations' loss of freedom to live honoring their cultural norms, the professor's narrative discourse ranges globally from Mexico City to Washington, D.C., San Francisco, Barcelona, Boston, Berlin, and China, familiar sites to Enrigue, who studied Communications at Mexico City's Universidad Iberoamericana, subsequently appointed Professor of Literature in the Department of Letters. He was Master of Arts in Latin American literature and professor at the University of Maryland, sojourner in Washington, D.C., honored guest at Berlin's 2004 International Literature Festival, and writer-in-residence at New York Public Research Library, 2011-2012.

Ishi is a Yahi Indian who in the course of the story undergoes a metamorphosis changing him from "last wild Indian in the United States" to a ghost that haunts then possesses the narrator. The professor-narrator tries to get free of, unknowingly to exorcize, the psychologically-engendered "demon" that afflicts him. This evil spirit is born of the pain and suffering inflicted upon Ishi by a white society which does not really know what to do with a man like Ishi, relegating him to living out his mortal existence as an exiled pariah. In the story's beguilingly constructed design, Ishi's socioeconomic banishment to solitude and isolation parallels the professor's writer's block, manifesting in inability to write a story he desperately wants to write, inspired by "an exhibition with photos of Ishi" he once saw displayed in the museum at the University of California, Berkeley (35). Attentively, he observes Ishi, a victim of starvation and dehydration who stirs his interest, but the pictorial representation of Ishi's plight attracts and repels him.

Key to appreciating "On the Death of the Author" is an image of a "boy who, having been bitten by a dog, had turned into a dog" (49). While the professor is retrieving memorable figural images of Ishi, he is gradually possessed by Ishi's disembodied soul. Meanwhile, Ishi's mangled body is raised from the dead in a double sense. As Ishi recovers his health, he is acculturated for his indigenous nature-oriented Indian culture is systematically displaced by modern civilization's materialism and conformism. The professor's narrative discourse transcends the sociological theme foregrounded in Ishi's acculturation and absorption into a racially-oriented hierarchy of societal stratification.

The professor persists, incited by his determination to compose a fictional piece portraying America's last wild Indian. Rejecting "pastiche, direct narrative, that abominable 'stream of consciousness,' diary entries, letters," he produces a meandering heartfelt account, overcoming frustration to finish his literary portrait of Ishi (35). "On the Death of the Author" resembles another of Enrigue's works. In *The Cemetery of Chairs,* Enrigue uses a variety of techniques—diaries, omniscient third-person narrators, and such themes as the African diaspora and disintegration of ethnic cultures and personal identity. The professor's dilemma may be traced to a geopolitical conflict that transpired ontologically without regard for aesthetics. Resembling a morally-freighted tale of mystery and imagination *à la* Edgar Allan Poe, the professor's tale has an arabesque quality, an exotic tincture that underscores the symbiotic relationship between storyteller and "wild Indian." In attempting to tell Ishi's story, the professor has to bridge a culturally-constructed lacuna created by the historic clash of indigenous American Yahi / Hopi culture and Anglo-European-American societal norms. Indeed, the professor asserts that "there is something in his tale—or in me—that turns it to mercury" (35). Mercury is a poisonous element, liquid and volatile, immediately sensitive to changes in temperature, particularly to heat. In large quantities of great magnitude and density, mercury generates a palpable atmosphere, including on Mercury, the planet closest to the Sun. Ishi is the last surviving member of the Yahi Indian tribes in northern California, which belong to a branch of the Hopi Indian tribes indigenous for eons to northeast Arizona. Archaeologists and anthropologists believe that the Hopi ancestral tree predates all other Native American Indian tribes. While the descendants of the original Hopi, who organized towns and lived together in houses atop the territorial plateaus now occupied by the U.S. state of Arizona, maintained their society as flourishing agriculturists (currently as proprietors of tourist attractions), the smaller, less numerous Yahi Indians were hunted down, their villages plundered by territorial expansionists who were motivated by their fervent belief in the doctrine of manifest destiny spawned by Charles Darwin's promulgation of a survival of the fittest theory. Early mention of the poisonous metal mercury in the fifth of the story's forty-four paragraphs of varying length signals symbolically the commencement of a subtextual undercurrent where the professor succeeds, after ten years of failure, in telling the postmodern epic story of "a grand finale," as he states in the first paragraph. Yet, this narratological-ly-engineered writing process leads inexorably to the "Death of the Author" (32, 33).

The professor, a paragon of Anglo-European culture, learns to appreciate Ishi's stoicism and deplores the tragedy and pathos of Ishi's capture by a county sheriff, "perhaps, the Wild West's last cowboy," who lifted Ishi, "threw him over the rump of his horse, and carried him to jail" (35). Intriguingly, Ishi officially assumes his identity as a societal ghost when the sheriff charitably dresses Ishi in "his [the sheriff's] own clothing" and asks his wife to prepare special meals for Ishi "so that he would not die of starvation before being handed over to the army, which was the standard procedure" (35). As the story progresses, Ishi's life achieves dignity owing to a Vodun-rooted bridge produced by the professor's gaze. Damballah-like, the professor sloughs his biases about ethnic / racial differences; the end result is that author and protagonist form a synergy. The professor-narrator's old mind-body dies, reborn to oneness of spiritual being with Ishi, whose Hopi mind-body died when Ishi was captured as a prisoner of war but whose spirit-being grew more powerful in captivity. Housed in a museum, Ishi is reborn as the professor-author's muse. As King Hamlet's disembodied spirit becomes Prince Hamlet's reason for living (and dying), so Ishi's ghostly existence dwells in the professorial author's mind-body.

A newcomer to Mexican fiction, María Isabel Aguirre graduated with a Bachelor of Arts degree in Spanish literature at the Universidad Estatal de Guayaquil in Guayaquil, capital of Guayas province, a former Spanish colony, 1534-1822, in the democratic republic of Ecuador. The first-person narrator in Aguirre's "Today, You Walk Along a Narrow Path" (2001) is a personage that may be seen to rarefy the tragic figures in Shakespeare's *Hamlet* by transcending traditional elements of plot and story and entering a stream of consciousness imbued with West African Vodun theological belief. The dramatized narrator is a transparent reflector of spiritual reality, a realm of communion with deceased family members. This protagonist walks along a pathway consecrated to the dead, a pathway leading to the hallowed ground of the town cemetery where myriad gravestones mark the crossroads where the narrator's family members passed over from the land of the living to the domain of the dead. The protagonist is at first startled to be greeted by the consecrated spirits of the dead. In a state of heightened intellectual, social, and religious exaltation, the Hamlet-like celebrant of ancient Vodun-Mexica ritual observance warms to the occasion, welcoming the encounters with the specters, paying homage to them as divinities whose presence proclaims continuity between the living and the dead. Signaling an enhancement of the modern Spanish language in which the story was written, Aguirre asserts African theological beliefs and practices, which align harmoniously with ancient Mexica rites and rituals dedicated to worship of nature divinities.

Aguirre's ghost-tale employs a first-person narrator to indicate a Hamlet-like body-spirit parting of the ways as his body slowly releases his soul. Disembodiment is a process occurring beyond the grasp of the conscious mind. To emphasize this slipping away, the narrator freely associates sensory perceptions of mind observing body's arrival at a "celebration of the Solemnity of All Saints" in the community of Huitzuco: candles glowing, food aromas, and "in the distance hills and cornfields" (1). Tiered images create a vivid impression of distance, both spatial and temporal.

Along the pathway, figures suddenly emerge in the dimensionless expanse of "'out there,'" such as the Hamlet-like narrator's uncle, a wanderer in the misty darkness for "'twenty years,'" who discloses "'we all feel bad after a while and long to come back here'" (2). He disappears as quickly as he appeared only to be succeeded by the nephew's Aunt Enedina, who enunciates the fate of "'Uncle Juan,'" buried long ago, "'killed because he stole some cattle and slept with another man's wife'" (3). She maintains the *chiaroscuro* of intersecting worlds whose boundaries shift with the shimmer of flickering candles—living and dead, past and present, dream and reality— inviting her Hamlet-like nephew "'Let's go eat with the others'" to avoid the "many lost souls wandering about'" (3). Likewise, the light of "yellow paper lanterns" in this netherworld is revealed to be "crowds" of individual persons (2, 3). Among the blurred "turmoil" of shadowy faces, intensities of light enable the narrator to recognize more relatives, his Uncle Nicolás and Aunt Adela, who traversed great distances to "greet" him (3). But when the Hamlet-figure turns, it is as Laertes that the narrator sees "father" figure Polonius, who in turn sees his Ophelia-like daughter "Elvinta" (3). In *Hamlet*, Polonius and Ophelia follow King Hamlet in death, making Laertes move ever closer to sharing Prince Hamlet's tragic fate, but only Prince Hamlet can see a

specter. The two fatherless sons merge as a unified consciousness that strad-
dles Laertes's materialistic body orientation and Prince Hamlet's mind-spirit
alignment. Prince Hamlet shares with Laertes confinement to filial knowledge and experience. For an instant, Laertes's ignorance of the spirit-world
intersects with Prince Hamlet's unfinished comprehension. Momentarily,
Aguirre's Hamlet-like narrator does not believe his eyes; his nearest and
dearest family members are present, yet they ignore him. Aguirre polarizes
the compounded Laertes / Hamlet specter's incredulity ("'It cannot be . . . it's
impossible.'") and the actual ontological difference between the living and
the dead.

The surprise ending indicates a great divide between the deceased narrator and his closest relatives, who are not yet dead. This living-versus-dead
polarity is evoked in an ontological conundrum. The phantom Hamlet-like
narrator feels ignored at that very moment when his father and daughter pay
their respects, laying "some fruit and a lit candle" at his tomb (3). Aguirre
harmonizes form and content, deftly building toward a climactic conclusion
that captures and conveys the diverging epistemological pathways of life and
death. The narrator experiences an epiphany, only indirectly arriving at
knowledge that he is dead; if he is dead, he cannot see or be seen, he thinks.
Paradoxically, he is dead and buried, yet he is doubly aware of his entombed
body and his sentient spirit-in-the-world.

Aguirre's ghost-story resonates harmoniously with *Hamlet* and *Pedro
Páramo*. The narrating nephew resembles Hamlet and Preciado. Uncle Juan
reincarnates Claudius and Páramo. Aunt Enedina re-embodies two women
who have been married by men motivated not by love, but by desires for
material gain, Queen Gertrude and Dolores Preciado, whom Claudius and
Pedro Páramo exploited. Gertrude abrogates her position as mother and is
Prince Hamlet's aunt when she weds Claudius. Aguirre's Uncle Nicolás and
Aunt Adela resemble Shakespeare's happily-married King Hamlet and
Queen Gertrude before their tragic demise. The unnamed father and daughter
at the end are symbols of Aguirre's father, to whom the story is dedicated,
and Aguirre herself. And yet, it is tempting to propose that the father and
daughter also symbolize Rulfo and Aguirre, who lay the fruits of their labors
of love on soulful Prince Hamlet's tomb and light a candle to honor the
memory of pioneering Afro-Latin connoisseur Shakespeare.

Contemporary Mexican fiction uplifts contact of the living with the dead
to ontological pinnacles of meaning about the nature of mind-body being.
Epistemologically, life's meaning encompasses an afterlife. Spectral dynamics resonate with these philosophical matters submerged in artistic matrices
that plait historical, political, social, and religious filaments that together
shape Mexican culture. Cultivated in a fertile Catholic groundwork in the
postcolonial era, contemporary Mexican life and literature are profoundly
influenced by West African Vodun belief in life and death as intersecting

states of being-in-the-world, Náhual veneration of nature deities, and Mexica worship of heroic masculine and feminine ancestral divinities. Comparable to Shakespeare,[11] Rulfo, Zavala, and Aguirre portray the father-son archetype as a metonym that symbolizes linkages engrained in oppositions: death / life, individual / society, village / empire, and good / evil. These literary masterpieces strongly suggest that Mexican nationhood will derive cohesion through meshing, not mangling ethnically-diverse ideas about the invisible spiritual bridge that conjoins life and death. Portrayals of Afro-Latino spirits by these contemporary Mexican literary artists benefit from four mutually-reinforcing theological traditions to assure Mexico's ongoing realization of the transformative power of a rich cultural heritage to offset the sway of historic geopolitical turmoil and bloodshed. Historically, bloodshed has meant carnage and killing in military offensives but the shedding of blood has also played an important role in Mexica religious beliefs and practices sanctioned by warrior-priests. As Hugh Thomas observes in *Conquest: Montezuma, Cortés, and the Fall of Old Mexico*, Mexica warrior culture showcased ritual blood sacrifice: "Priests were ascetic celibates of high standing. Two high priests commanded them: one to serve Huitzilopochtli, the other . . . the still very important deity, Tlaloc, god of rain. Both were named by the Emperor. . . . Their bodies dyed black, their hair long, their ears tattered by offerings of blood, priests were immensely influential" (12).

Álvaro Enrigue's narratological aesthetics probes into the controversial sociopolitical issue of assimilation and acculturation of ethnic minorities into the dominant society. The psychological and philosophical mind-soul displacement of the professor-author as he absorbs the mind-soul of Ishi calls to mind the rather controversial juxtaposition of George Harris and Uncle Tom in Harriet Beecher Stowe's *Uncle Tom's Cabin*. Many of Stowe's African-American readers have been known to voice strong objections to this nineteenth-century novel's depiction of both George Harris and Uncle Tom because their patently praiseworthy characteristics frequently represent Non-African Anglo-European cultural values. Enrigue's "On the Death of the Author" evokes some of the pain and suffering experienced by ethnic and cultural minorities who are forcibly made to sacrifice their familial, ancestral, or other cultural heritage. Brilliantly Enrigue portrays the lifelong torment, tribulations, and last ordeal of Ishi as he gradually loses his self-identity, as observed through the sensitive articulate narrative discourse of the empathetic American professor-narrator. Enrigue's compelling motif in "On the Death of the Author" is cultural loss and homelessness. The storytelling professor-narrator experiences joy and sadness because Ishi's successful assimilation—Ishi is no longer a "wild" Indian—coincides with the author's sense of homelessness as a professor in the academic discipline of history.

While Ishi changes his identity from Native American Indian to acculturated American museum curator, the narrator, whose occupation is as a dedicated professor of history, experiences his own demise because Ishi's loss of ethnic identity symbolizes the devaluation of vast epochs in the history of humankind. As a museum curator, Ishi has become less important as a human being than the relics that will survive him. Ultimately, "On the Death of the author" decries inhumane materialism while at the same time celebrating the mind-soul creativity, intellect, imagination, and moral courage through which storytellers, authors, and museum curators endeavor to advance the body of humanity.

NOTES

1. Juan Rulfo observes, "Chichimecas" in Náhuatl means "dogs without muzzles" (*Cuadernos* 164; my trans.).
2. "New Spain" was legalized by Spain's Colonization Laws of 1573.
3. Vodun theological beliefs and practices originated in Black Africa before 6000 BC.
4. My 2001 article "Native Vision" discusses conflicting linguistic-cultural allegiances.
5. Until Dante Alighieri (1265-1320), European authors wrote in Latin; for example, see my article on "Hrotsvit (Roswitha, Hrotswitha) of Gandersheim (932-1002),"which describes the life and works of the first Germanic Saxon poet (Watanabe 341-43).
6. Black African Moors settled in Mediterranean Europe, especially Spain and Italy.
7. Ilan Stavans notes that Juan Rulfo "acknowledged the influence of Norwegian authors such as Knut Hamsun (né Knut Pederson) and Selma Lagerlöf" (xiv). Wolfgang Vogt discusses Juan Rulfo's 1930s and 1940s reading of Knut Hamsun (65-69), Selma Lagerlöf (71-74), Danish novelist Jen Peter Jacobsen (61-64), and Icelandic novelist Halldor Laxness (75-79).
8. Chapter 24 in my book *Beloved Image* discusses *Pedro Páramo* in the "Ultrasound" section on consanguinity (Watanabe 267-315).
9. Spain retained "Aztec nobility" in "positions of power" (*tlatoques* and *caciques*) to conceal Spain's hegemony (Menchaca 50).
10. In 1862, Mexican troops defeated French armies at Puebla, near Mexico City, a battle known as "Cinco de mayo." The toy soldier symbol also points to Napoleon's 1808 invasion of Spain.
11. Sumie Okada observes, "Alerted and motivated by the appearance of his late father's ghost," Prince Hamlet achieves his "individualistic objective" of "expelling all the evil from his court" (6, 8). As Harold Bloom observes, "Hamlet of Act 5 is a changed man . . . . no longer haunted by his father's ghost" (229).

WORKS CITED

Aguirre, María Isabel. "Today, You Walk along a Narrow Path." Translated by Rebecca Huerta. *Three Messages and a Warning: Contemporary Mexican Short Stories of the Fantastic.* Ed. Eduardo Jiménez Mayo and Chris N. Brown. Easthampton, Massachusetts: Small Beer Press, 2011. 1-3.

Bloom, Harold. "An Essay." In *The Tragedy of Hamlet: Prince of Denmark*. The Annotated Shakespeare. By William Shakespeare. Edited by Burton Raffel. New Haven: Yale University Press, 2003. 229-43.

Drachler, Jacob. *African Heritage: Intimate Views of the Black Africans from Life, Lore, and Literature.* New York: Crowell-Collier, 1963.

Enrigue, Álvaro. "Sobre la muerte del autor / On the Death of the Author." Translated by C. M. Mayo. *Best of Contemporary Mexican Fiction.* Edited by Álvaro Uribe with Olivia Sears. Champaign and London: Dalkey Archive Press, 2009. 32-55.

Gandhi, Leela. *Postcolonial Theory: A Critical Introduction.* New York: Columbia University Press, 1998.

Herskovits, Melville J. *Cultural Dynamics.* New York: Knopf, 1964.

Holy Bible: New King James Version. Tulsa: Honor Books, 1997.

Lizardi, José Joaquin Fernández de Lizardi. *The Mangy Parrot: The Life and Times of Periquillo Sarniento Written by Himself for His Children.* Translated by David Frye. Indianapolis: Hackett, 2004.

———. *El Periquillo Sarniento.* New York: Appleton-Century-Crofts, 1952.

Menchaca, Martha. *Recovering History, Constructing Race: The Indian, Black, and White Roots of Mexican Americans.* Austin: University of Texas Press, 2001.

Okada, Sumie. *Japanese Writers and the West.* New York: Palgrave Macmillan, 2003.

Raffel, Burton, ed. Introduction. *The Tragedy of Hamlet: Prince of Denmark.* By William Shakespeare. New Haven: Yale University Press, 2003. xiii-xxix.

Rulfo, Juan. *The Burning Plain and Other Stories.* 1967. Translated by George D. Schade. Austin: University of Texas Press, 2008.

———. *Los Cuadernos de Juan Rulfo.* Edited by Clara Aparicio de Rulfo and Yvette Jiménez de Báez. Mexico City: Era, 1995.

———. *Pedro Páramo.* 1994. Translated by Margaret Sayers Peden. Evanston: Northwestern University Press, 1994.

Shakespeare, William. *The Tragedy of Hamlet: Prince of Denmark.* The Annotated Shakespeare. Edited by Burton Raffel. New Haven: Yale University Press, 2003.

Starkie, Walter. Introduction. *Don Quixote of La Mancha.* By Miguel de Cervantes Saavedra. Translated by Walter Starkie. New York: Signet, 1964.

Stavans, Ilan. Introduction. *The Plain in Flames.* Translated by Ilan Stavans with Harold Augenbraum. Austin: University of Texas Press, 2012. Ix-xvi.

Thomas, Hugh. *Conquest: Montezuma, Cortés, and the Fall of Old Mexico.* 1993. New York: Simon and Schuster, 2005.

Vogeley, Nancy J. *Lizardi and the Birth of the Novel in Spanish America.* Gainesville: University Press of Florida, 2001.

Vogt, Wolfgang. *Juan Rulfo y el Sur de Jalisco: Aspectos de su vida y obra.* Guadalajara: El Colegio de Jalisco, 1992; Agata, 1994.

Watanabe, Nancy Ann. *Beloved Image: The Drama of W. B. Yeats 1865-1939.* Lanham, New York, London: University Press of America, 1996.

———. "Hrotsvit (Roswitha; Hrotswitha) of Gandersheim." *New Catholic Encyclopedia: Supplement 2011: Art, Music, and Literature.* 2 vols. Edited by Robert L. Fastiggi. Washington: Catholic University of America Press; Detroit: Gale, 2011. 2: 341-43.

———. "Native Vision: Yeats's Tower (*The Dreaming of the Bones*) and Walcott's Harbor (*Dream on Monkey Mountain*)." *W. B. Yeats and Postcolonialism.* Edited by Deborah Fleming. West Cornwall: Locust Hill Press, 2001. 143-65.

Zavala, Hernán Lara. "A golpe de martilla" / "Hammering Away." Translated by Pamela Carmell. *Best of Contemporary Mexican Fiction.* Edited by Álvaro Uribe with Olivia Sears. Champaign: Dalkey Archive, 2009. 434–49.

Afterword

First and foremost, I express my appreciation of the anonymous referees whose written evaluations of the excerpted chapters in my book manuscript, done in accordance with the academic blind review process, prevented errors and articulated conceptual and thematic strengths that they discerned in my work. Furthermore, I am grateful to Petra Rivera-Rideau, Jennifer Jones, and Tianna Paschel for reading my comparative analysis paper now unveiled as the third chapter in this book.

At the Press, I thank Holly Buchanan, assistant acquisitions editor, and her assistant Emma Richard at Hamilton Books; Laura Chappell, assistant production editor at Rowman & Littlefield; Della Vache, assistant managing editor at Rowman & Littlefield; and president Julie Kirsch and Beverly Shellem, senior production editor, formerly of University Press of America (UPA, established 1975), now Rowman & Littlefield (inaugurated 1949; acquired by UPA in 1988), for enabling *African Heartbeat* to find a pathway amid the intricacies of the publication process. We recognize the hundreds of individual scholars and college, university, and public research libraries without whose encouraging letters, emails, telephone calls, and financial support of my UPA books, *Beloved Image* on the poetical Irish plays of William Butler Yeats and *Love Eclipsed* on the postcolonial American fiction of Joyce Carol Oates, *African Heartbeat: Transatlantic Literary and Cultural Dynamics* could not have been published by Hamilton Books (founded 2003), an imprint of Rowman & Littlefield.

My library research is supplemented by my firsthand knowledge of multicultural diversity, which includes African, American, African-American, and Mexican culture, and in addition, national, state, and municipal public safety services. In this regard, I would like to salute, personally and professionally, in no particular order, some unforgettable colleagues, governmental officials, co-workers, even K-12 classmates: Melvin B. Tolson, Jr., Derek Walcott, Janet Clayton, Harry Murphy, James Justus, Jocelyn Gilbertson Harvey, George Bluestone, Mary Reichardt, Gregory Tague, Rose De Angelis, Raymond-Jean Frontain, Akhter Ahsen, Danette DiMarco, Françoise Ghillebaert, Gloria McMillan, Louise Richards, Linda Leaver, Mark Gazeley, Janice Spleth, Sylvia Wilson, Jan Rutherford, Jerry Bridges, Amanda Pirog, Henry Wonham, James Gray, Kelly Gerald, Faye Hammill, Carla Clift, Fatima Barnes, Faye Watkins, Jean Greene, Cynthia Charles, Linda Orzel, Jessie Smith, Ruth Hodges, Paul Blackmon, Monika Rhue, Paulette Johnson, LaVerne McLaughlin, Linda Carty, Safiya Noble, Karida L. Brown, Vladimir Ashkenazy, John C. Mayer, Mary Mikkelsen, Carolyn Johnson Allen, Moses Nkondo, Chaman Sahni, Glenn Selander, George H. W. Bush, Patty Murray, Maria Cantwell, Jay Inslee, Patrick Fitzsimons, Gil Kerlikowske, Norm Rice, John Emmerson, Paul Valenti, Ruby Harris, Luther Norman, Ben Alexander, Darnell White, Kendall Young, Ric Ochoa, Renée Treadwell, Al Gage, Ben Wright, Richard Korpela, Kal Brauner, Linda Garbini Manning, Lund Chin, Clarence Seeliger, Cherie Tucker, Barbara Nagaoka, Teresa Anderson, Jeanette L. Herbison, Lily Tse, Marion Budinich (Keith) Bergstrom, Jean Whitcomb, Alice Kihara, Wanda Jackson, Gary Robertson, and many others. For judicious consideration in accommodating me as an academic while acquainting me with hitherto unfamiliar aspects of the American organizational experience, I thank Adam Corson, Kay McGau, Sheldon Z. Goldberg, Lori Cross, Barbara Jackson Strayer, Daijiro Ueda, Richard Miyata, Michael Erickson, Myra Imami, Madison Pascua, and their prodigious staffs and colleagues. Certainly, *African Heartbeat* is a better book because of the encouragement and advice of these and many other friends.

My labors as a scholar working in isolation for long stretches of time make me rather grateful for the intellectual esprit de corps of fellow contributors of chapters to faculty compiled/edited academic books. I am appreciative of colleagues, most of whom I never met, in these peer reviewed books and academic journals, including *W. B. Yeats and Postcolonialism*, ed. Deborah Fleming (Cristina J. Thaut, Spurgeon Thompson, Eugene O'Brien, Raphael Ingelbien, Richard Rankin Russell, Alexander C. Irvine, Mark Mossman, Derek Hand, Cara B. McClintock, Carrie Etter, Martin McKinsey, Christopher T. Malone, Rached Khalifa, Rebecca Weaver [Hightower]); *Between Human and Divine: The Catholic Vision in Contemporary Literature*, ed. Mary R. Reichardt (Patricia L. Schnapp, Daniel S. Lenoski, Robert P. Lewis, Eamon Maher, Salvador A. Oropesa, Nan Metzger, Wendy A. Weaver, Ed Block, Gary M. Bouchard, Michael G. Brennan, J. C. Whitehouse, Stephen McInerney, Davin Heckman, Dominic Manganiello, Meoghan B. Cronin); *Origins of English Dramatic Modernism, 1870-1914*, ed. Gregory F. Tague and Daniel Meyer-Dinkgräfe (Benjamin Poore, Kelly Jones, Diane Dubois, Felicia J. Ruff, Frances L. Piper, Timothy Carlo Matos, Patricia D. Denison,

Allan Pero, Franc Chamberlain, Evanthia Kasouraki, Miriam M. Chiriko, Lance Norman, Jennifer Plastow); *Italian Americana, Special Issue on World War II and Beyond*, ed. Carole Bonomo Albright (Rose De Angelis, Stefano Luconi); *A Talent for the Particular: Critical Essays on R. K. Narayan*, ed. Raymond-Jean Frontain and Basudeb Chakraborti (Sankar Sinha, Baisali Hui, Chirantan Sarkar, Bryan Hull, Debiprasad Bhattacharya, Binayak Roy, Urmila Chakraborty, Niladri Chatterjee, Kalyan Chatterjee, Daniel W. Ross, Anghuman Kar, Himadri Lahiri, Amit Bhattacharya, Leena Sarkar); and *Inhabited by Stories: Critical Essays on Tales Retold*, ed. Nancy A. Barta-Smith and Danette DiMarco (Magali Cornier Michael, Grant Bain, Karen M. Cardozo, Laura Keigan, Karley Adney, LaDelle Davenport, Cheryl A. Wilson, Valerie Estelle Frankel, Shannon L. Reed, Debarati Bandyopadhyay, Vandana Saxena, Gary Totten, Barbara Roche Rico, Victor Velázquez, Andrew Higl).

I am grateful to the hundreds of faculty scholars, individuals, and librarians who have supported the publication of my scholarly books, including the following libraries: Auburn University at Montgomery, Alabama; Auburn University, Auburn University, Alabama; University of Alabama, Tuscaloosa; Anchorage School District, Alaska; University of Arkansas, Fayetteville; Northern Arizona University, Flagstaff; Arizona State University, Tempe; University of Arizona Libraries, Tucson; Saint John's Seminary College at Camarillo, California; California Institute of the Arts, Santa Clarita; Stanford University Libraries, Stanford, California; California State University, Northridge; California State Polytechnic University, Pomona; University of California, Irvine; University of California, Los Angeles; University of California, Santa Barbara; Loyola Marymount University, Los Angeles, California; San Francisco State University, San Francisco, California; University of Colorado, Denver; University of Colorado, Boulder; Colorado State University, Fort Collins; University of Denver, Denver, Colorado; University of Connecticut, Storrs; Yale University, New Haven, Connecticut; Wesleyan University, Middletown, Connecticut; Library of Congress, Washington, D.C.; Georgetown University, Washington, D.C.; American University, Washington, D.C.; Catholic University of America, Washington, D.C.; University of Delaware, Newark; Florida State University, Tallahassee; University of South Florida, Tampa; Nova Southeastern University, Ft. Lauderdale, Florida; University of North Florida, Jacksonville; University of Central Florida, Orlando; University of Miami, Coral Gables, Florida; Emory University, Atlanta, Georgia; University of Georgia, Athens; Atlanta University Center, Atlanta, Georgia; Atlanta University Center, Georgia; Augusta College, Augusta, Georgia; Georgia State University, Atlanta; Boise State University, Boise, Idaho; University of Idaho, Moscow, Idaho; Iowa State University, Ames, Iowa; Grinnell College, Grinnell, Iowa; Loras College, Dubuque, Iowa; DePaul University, Chicago, Illinois; Southern Illinois University, Carbondale; Loyola University of Chicago, Illinois; University of Illinois, Champaign-Urbana; University of Notre Dame, Notre Dame, Indiana; Kansas State University, Manhattan; University of Kansas, Lawrence; University of Kentucky, Lexington; University of Massachusetts; Brandeis University, Waltham, Massachusetts; Wheaton College, Norton, Massachusetts; University of Massachusetts, Amherst; Boston College, Chestnut Hill, Massachusetts; Emerson College, Boston, Massachusetts; Bates College, Lewiston, Maine; University of Maryland Libraries, College Park, Maryland; United States Naval Academy, Annapolis, Maryland; University of Michigan, Ann Arbor; Carleton College, Northfield, Minnesota; University of Mississippi, University, Mississippi; University of Missouri, Columbia; University of North Carolina Libraries, Greensboro; University of North Carolina, Chapel Hill; North Carolina State University, Raleigh; University of Nebraska, Lincoln; Creighton University, Omaha, Nebraska; Hastings College, Hastings, Nebraska; Princeton University, Princeton, New Jersey; University of Nevada Libraries, Las Vegas; State University of New York, Buffalo; Public Library Research Library, New York, New York; State University of New York College at Brockport; State University of New York College at Cortland; Columbia University, New York, New York; State University of New York College at New Paltz; State University of New York, Albany; Hartwick College, Oneonta, New York; University of Akron, Akron, Ohio; University of Cincinnati, Cincinnati, Ohio; Case Western Reserve University, Cleveland, Ohio; Ohio State University, Columbus, Ohio; Ohio University, Athens, Ohio; University of Toledo, Toledo, Ohio; Youngstown State University, Youngstown, Ohio; Oklahoma State University, Stillwater; University of Tulsa, Tulsa, Oklahoma; University of Oklahoma, Norman; University of Oregon Libraries, Eugene; Willamette University, Salem, Oregon; University of Pittsburgh, Pennsylvania; Swarthmore College, Swarthmore, Pennsylvania; Dickinson College, Carlisle, Pennsylvania; Lehigh University, Bethlehem, Pennsylvania; Bucknell University, Lewisburg, Pennsylvania; Pennsylvania State University, University Park; Free Library of Philadelphia, Pennsylvania; Washington and Jefferson College, Washington, Pennsylvania; College of Charleston, Charleston, South Carolina; University of South Carolina Libraries, Columbia; University of South Dakota, Vermillion; Vanderbilt University, Memphis, Tennessee; Tennessee Technological University, Cookeville; University of Tennessee, Chattanooga; Middle Tennessee State University, Murfreesboro; University of Texas Libraries, Austin; Stephen F. Austin University, Nacagdoches, Texas; Baylor University Libraries, Waco, Texas; Texas Southern University, Houston; Brigham Young University, Provo, Utah; University of Utah, Salt Lake City; George Mason University, Fairfax, Virginia; Old Dominion University, Norfolk, Virginia; Seattle Public Library, Seattle, Washington; King County Library System, Issaquah, Washington; Central Washington University, Ellensburg; Eastern Washington State University, Cheney; Whitman College, Walla Walla, Washington; University of Wisconsin, Milwaukee; West Virginia University, Morgantown; York University, North York, Ontario, Canada; McMaster University, Hamilton, Ontario, Canada; University of Western Ontario, London, Ontario, Canada; University of Waterloo, Ontario, Canada; University of Leeds, Yorkshire, England; University of Glasgow, Scotland.

St. Martin's College, Lacy, Washington; University of Alberta, Edmonton, Canada; University of Victoria, British Columbia, Canada; University of Nevada, Reno; University of California, Davis; University of California Libraries, Berkeley; University of Wyoming, Laramie; Los Angeles Public Library; University of Southern California, Los Angeles; University of California, Riverside; California State University, Sacramento; College of St. Benedict / St. John's University, Collegeville, Minnesota; University of Nebraska, Omaha; Missouri State University, Springfield; Ripon College, Ripon, Wisconsin; University of Illinois, Springfield; University of Wisconsin, Oshkosh; William Rainey Harper College, Palatine, Illinois; Andrews University, Berrien Springs, Michigan; Northeastern Illinois University, Chicago; St. Louis University, St. Louis, Missouri; Texas A & M University, College Station; University of Missouri, St. Louis; Central Michigan University Libraries, Mt. Pleasant; Eastern Michigan University Libraries, Ypsilanti; Hathi Trust Digital Library, Ann Arbor, Michigan; Indiana University, Bloomington; Indiana State University, Terre Haute; Indiana University-Purdue University Fort Wayne, Fort Wayne, Indiana; Lone Star College System, Houston, Texas; Stephen F. Austin State University, Nacogdoches, Texas; Texas A & M International University, Laredo; University of Houston, Houston, Texas; University of Utah, Provo; Western Michigan University, Kalamazoo; Del Mar College, Corpus Christi, Texas; Oberlin College, Oberlin, Ohio; Vanderbilt University, Nashville, Tennessee; Western Kentucky University, Bowling Green, Kentucky; Western University, London, Ontario, Canada; Cleveland Public Library, Cleveland, Ohio; John Carroll University, University Heights, Ohio; Louisiana State University, Baton Rouge; McMaster University, Hamilton, Ontario, Canada; University of Alabama at Birmingham; Tulane University, New Orleans, Louisiana; University of New Orleans, Louisiana; University of Toronto, Ontario, Canada; Appalachian State University, Boone, North Carolina; Clemson University Libraries, Clemson, South Carolina; Erie Community College, Williamsville, New York; Frank and Laura Lewis Library, Lagrange, Georgia; Indiana University of Pennsylvania, Indiana, Pennsylvania; University of North Georgia, Dahlonega; University of Pittsburgh, Pennsylvania; University of Rochester, New York; University of West Florida, Pensacola; University of West Georgia, Carrollton; Cornell University, Ithaca, New York; Syracuse University, New York; University of Virginia, Charlottesville; Washington and Lee University, Lexington, Virginia; American University, Washington, D.C.; Columbia University in the City of New York; Duke University Libraries, Durham, North Carolina; Fordham University, Bronx, New York; George Mason University, Fairfax, Virginia; Neumann University, Aston, Pennsylvania; Temple University Libraries, Philadelphia, Pennsylvania; University of Pennsylvania Libraries, Philadelphia; University of South Carolina, System Library Service, Columbia; Villanova University, Villanova, Pennsylvania; Virginia Commonwealth University, Richmond; William Paterson University of New Jersey, Wayne, New Jersey; Bates College Library, Lewiston, Maine; Brandeis University Library, Waltham, Massachusetts; Colby College, Waterville, Maine; Colby College Share Collection, Waterville, Maine; Flagler College, St. Augustine, Florida; Harvard College Library Technical Services, Cambridge, Massachusetts; New York Institute of Technology, Old Westbury, New York; Old Dominion University, Norfolk, Virginia; Rivier University, Nashua, New Hampshire; Salve Regina University Library, Newport, Rhode Island; Smith College, Northampton, Massachusetts; Stony Brook University, New York; University of Maine at Augusta, Maine; University of North Florida, Carpenter Library, Jacksonville; University of Southern Maine Lewiston, Maine; Wesleyan University, Middletown, Connecticut; Bangor Public Library, Bangor, Maine; University of Central Florida, Orlando, Florida; University of South Florida, Tampa, Florida; Brigham Young University-Hawaii, Laie, Hawaii; Broward College, Ft. Lauderdale, Florida; Florida International University, North Miami, Florida; Nova Southeastern University/ASLRITC/ILL, Ft. Lauderdale, Florida; Memorial University Newfoundland, Elizabeth II, St. Johns, Newfoundland, Canada; The British Library, On Demand, Wetherby, West Yorkshire, England; Libris, Stockholm, Sweden; Danish Union Catalogue and Danish National Bibliography, Ballerup, Denmark; University Library of Southern Denmark–Odense University Library, Odense M, Denmark; Bibliothek der Freien Universität Berlin, Germany; Bibliothèque nationale de France, Paris; Hochschul-und Landesbibliothek Rhein Main, Rheinstraße, Wiesbaden, Germany; Niedersächsische Staats-und Universitätsbibliothek Göttingen, Göttingen, Germany; Universitätsbibliothek Bayreuth, Germany; Universitätsbibliothek Freiburg, Freiburg/Breisgau, Germany; Bayerische Staatsbibliothek, München, Germany; Universitätsbibliothek Regensburg, Germany; Zentralbibliothek, Zürich, Switzerland; American College of Greece, Athens; Hong Kong Baptist University, Kowloon; American University of Sharjah, United Arab Emirates; University of New England, Armidale, Australia; Monash University Library, Clayton, Australia; University of Melbourne Libraries, Parkville, Australia; Buffalo State–State University of New York College at Buffalo, Buffalo, New York; Universiteitsbibliotheek Leiden/Leiden University Library, Leiden, Netherlands; University of Regina, Regina, Canada; California Institute of the Arts, Valencia; Auraria Library, University of Colorado Denver, Colorado; University of Guelph, Ontario, Canada; Queen's University Documents Library, Kingston, Ontario, Canada; University of Scranton, Pennsylvania; Université de Québec à Montréal, Canada; Wake Forest University, Winston-Salem, North Carolina; Johns Hopkins University, Baltimore, Maryland; New York Public Library System; Rutgers University, New Brunswick, New Jersey; Western Connecticut State University, Danbury; Assumption College, Worcester, Massachusetts; Atlantic Union College Library, South Lancaster, Massachusetts; University of North Carolina, Wilmington; Eckerd College, St. Petersburg, Florida; University of Miami, Coral Gables, Florida; University of Aberdeen, Old Aberdeen, Scotland; University of Sheffield, England; University of Cambridge, England; University of London Senate House Library, England; Staatsbibliothek zu Berlin Preußischer Kulturbesitz-Haus Potsdamer Straße, Germany; TU Berlin–Universitätsbibliothek; Universitäts-und Landesbibliothek Sachsen-Anhalt/Zentrale, Halle Saale, Germany; Universitätsbibliothek Gießen, Germany; Universitätsbibliothek Johann Christian Senckenberg Zentralbibliothek, Frankfurt/Main, Frankfurt, Germany; Sächsische Landesbibliothek-Staats-und Universitätsbibliothek Dresden, Germany; Universitätsbibliothek Bamberg, Bamberg, Germany; Universitätsbibliothek Mannheim, Germany; Universitätsbibliothek Würzburg, Germany; Universitätsbibliothek der Eberhard Karls Universität, Tübingen, Germany; Württembergische Landesbibliothek, Stuttgart, Germany; Biblioteca de la Universidad Complutense de Madrid, España, Madrid, Spain; Universitätsbibliothek Basel, Switzerland; Universitätsbibliothek Passau, Germany; Universitätsbibliothek Regensburg, Germany; Universitätsbibliothek, Bern, Switzerland; The Chinese University of Hong Kong, Shatin, N.T.; Australian National University, Canberra; University of Melbourne Libraries, Parkville, Australia.

I reserve this space for historically Black college and university libraries, including Alabama State University, Albany State University, Acorn State University, Allen University, American Baptist College, Arkansas Baptist College, Atlanta University Center, Benedict College, Bennett College, Bethune-Cookman University, Bluefield State College, Bowie State University, Central State University, Cheyney University of Pennsylvania, Claflin University, Clark Atlanta University, Coahoma Community College, Concordia College Alabama, Delaware State University, Denmark Technical College, Dillard University, Edward Waters College, Elizabeth City State University, Fayetteville State University, Fisk University, Florida A & M University, Florida Memorial University, Grambling State University, Hampton University, Harris-Stowe State University, Hinds Community College Utica Campus, Howard University, Huston-Tillotson University, Interdenominational Theological Center, J. F. Drake State Community and Technical College, Jackson State University, Jarvis Christian College, Johnson C. Smith University, Kentucky State University, Lane College, Langston University, Lawson State Community College, LeMoyne-Owen College, Lincoln University

(Missouri), Lincoln University (Pennsylvania), Livingstone College, Mehar-
ry Medical College, Miles College, Mississippi Valley State University,
Morehouse College, Morehouse School of Medicine, Morgan State Univer-
sity, Morris College, Norfolk State University, North Carolina A & T State
University, North Carolina Central University, Oakwood University, Paul
Quinn College, Philander Smith College, Prairie View A & M University,
Saint Augustine's University, Savannah State University, Shaw University,
Shelton State Community College, South Carolina State University, South-
ern University and A & M College, Southern University at Shreveport,
Southern University New Orleans, Spelman College, St. Philips College,
Tennessee State University, Texas College, Texas Southern University, Tou-
galoo College, Trenholm State Community College, Tuskegee University,
University of Arkansas at Pine Bluff, University of Maryland Eastern Shore,
University of the District of Columbia, University of the Virgin Islands,
Virginia State University, Virginia Union University, Voorhees College,
West Virginia State University, Wilberforce University, Winston-Salem
State University, Xavier University of Louisiana.

Bibliography

Adams, John R. *Harriet Beecher Stowe*. Boston: Twayne, 1989.

Aguirre, María Isabel. "Today, You Walk along a Narrow Path." Translated by Rebecca Huerta. *Three Messages and a Warning: Contemporary Mexican Short Stories of the Fantastic*. Edited by Eduardo Jiménez Mayo and Chris N. Brown. Easthampton, Massachusetts: Small Beer Press, 2011. 1-3.

Ammons, Elizabeth, and Susan Belasco. Introduction. *Approaches to Teaching Stowe's Uncle Tom's Cabin*. New York: Modern Language Association of America, 2000. 1-4.

Bloom, Harold. "An Essay." In *The Tragedy of Hamlet: Prince of Denmark*. The Annotated Shakespeare. By William Shakespeare. Edited by Burton Raffel. New Haven: Yale University Press, 2003. 229-43.

Brandon, George. *Santeria from Africa to the New World: The Dead Sell Memories: Blacks in the Diaspora*. Bloomington: Indiana University Press, 1997.

Burris, Andrew. "The Browsing Reader. Review of *Jonah's Gourd Vine*." *Critical Essays on Zora Neale Hurston*. Edited by Gloria L. Cronin. New York: G. K. Hall, 1998. 35-36.

Cartwright, Keith. "'To Walk with the Storm': Oya as the Transformative 'I' of Zora Neale Hurston's Afro-Atlantic Callings." *American Literature* 78, no. 4 (December 2006): 741-67.

Cassidy, Thomas. "Janie's Rage: The Dog and the Storm in *Their Eyes Were Watching God*." *CLA Journal: A Quarterly of the College Language Association* 36, no. 3 (March 1993): 260-69.

Cobley, Paul. "The Paranoid Style in Narrative: The Anxiety of Storytelling After 9/11." *Narratologia: Intermediality and Storytelling*. Berlin, DEU: Walter de Gruyter, 2010. ProQuest ebrary. 24 June 2015. 99-121.

Collins, Derek. "The Myth and Ritual of Ezili Freda in Hurston's *Their Eyes Were Watching God*." *Western Folklore* 55, no. 2 (Spring 1996): 137-54.

Cronin, Gloria L., ed. *Critical Essays on Zora Neale Hurston*. New York: G. K. Hall, 1998.

Curren, Erik. "Should Their Eyes Have Been Watching God? Hurston's Use of Religious Experience and Gothic Horror." *African American Review* 29, no. 1 (1995): 17-24.

Curry, Mary Cuthrell. *Living Gods of Haiti*. Kingston: McPherson, 1970.

Deren, Maya. *Divine Horsemen: Living Gods of Haiti*. New York: Vanguard, 1953.

Desmangles, Leslie G. *The Faces of the Gods: Vodou and Roman Catholicism in Haiti*. Chapel Hill and London: University of North Carolina Press, 1992.

Deutsch, Stephanie. *You Need a Schoolhouse: Booker T. Washington, Julius Rosenwald, and the Building of Schools for the Segregated South*. Evanston: Northwestern University Press, 2011.

Dorsey, Lilith. *Voodoo and Afro-Caribbean Paganism*. Foreword by Isaac Bonewits. New York: Citadel Press, Kensington Publishing Group, 2005.

Drachler, Jacob. *African Heritage: Intimate Views of the Black Africans from Life, Lore, and Literature.* New York: Crowell-Collier, 1963.

Enemy of the State. Directed by Tony Scott. Written by David Marconi. Costumes Designed by Marlene Stewart. Touchstone Pictures / Buena Vista, 1998. January 2, 2014. Television.

Enrigue, Álvaro. "Sobre la muerte del autor / On the Death of the Author." Translated by C. M. Mayo. *Best of Contemporary Mexican Fiction.* Edited by Álvaro Uribe with Olivia Sears. Champaign and London: Dalkey Archive Press, 2009. 32-55.

Fama, Chief Àiná Adéwálé-Somadhi. *Fundamentals of the Yorùbá Religion Òrìsà Worship.* San Bernardino: Ilé Òrúnmìlà Publications, 1993.

Ford, Sarah. "Necessary Chaos in Hurston's *Their Eyes Were Watching God.*" *CLA Journal: A Quarterly of the College Language Association* 43, no. 4 (June 2000): 407-19.

Gandhi, Leela. *Postcolonial Theory: A Critical Introduction.* New York: Columbia University Press, 1998.

Gates, Henry Louis, Jr. Afterword. *Seraph on the Suwanee: A Novel.* 1948. By Zora Neale Hurston. Foreword by Hazel V. Carby. New York: Harper Perennial, 1991.

Gettysburg. Produced and directed by Tony Scott and Ridley Scott. History Channel, 2011. Television.

Gikandi, Simon. Editor's Column. "The Fragility of Languages." *PMLA* 130 (Jan. 2015): 9-14.

Gioia, Ted. *The History of Jazz.* New York: Oxford University Press, 1997.

Giscard d'Estaing, Valéry. Interview. Charlie Rose Show. Public Broadcasting System. New York. June 4, 2015. Television.

Glaser, Ben. "Folk Iambics: Prosody, Vestiges, and Sterling Brown's Outline for the Study of the Poetry of American Negroes." *PMLA* 129 (May 2014): 417-34.

Harris, Susan K. Introduction. *The Minister's Wooing.* By Harriet Beecher Stowe. New York: Penguin, 1999. vii-xxiii.

Hedrick, Joan. *Harriet Beecher Stowe: A Life.* New York: Oxford University Press, 1994.

Herskovits, Melville J. *The American Negro: A Study in Racial Crossing.* Bloomington: Indiana University Press, 1938.

―――. *Cultural Dynamics.* Abridged from *Cultural Anthropology.* 1947. Preface by Joseph H. Greenberg. New York: Alfred A. Knopf, 1964.

Herzog, Kristin. "*Uncle Tom's Cabin* and *Incidents in the Life of a Slave Girl*: The Issue of Violence." *Approaches to Teaching Stowe's Uncle Tom's Cabin.* Edited by Elizabeth Ammons and Susan Belasco. New York: Modern Language Association of America, 2000. 132-41.

Holloway, Joseph E., ed. *Africanisms in American Culture.* Bloomington and Indianapolis: Indiana University Press, 1990.

Holy Bible: New King James Version. Tulsa: Honor Books, 1997.

Holy Bible. Old and New Testaments. King James Version. New York: Books, 1951.

Hubbard, Dolan. "'... Ah said Ah'd save de text for you'": Recontextualizing the Sermon to Tell (Her)story in Zora Neale Hurston's *Their Eyes Were Watching God."* *Critical Essays on Zora Neale Hurston.* Edited by Gloria L. Cronin. New York: G. K. Hall, 1998. 100-113.

Hughes, Langston. "I, Too, Sing America." 1925. *The Collected Poems.* New York: Knopf, 2007. 46.

―――. *The Big Sea.* New York: Hill and Wang, 1940.

Hurston, Zora Neale. *Jonah's Gourd Vine.* 1934. Edited by Henry Louis Gates, Jr. Foreword by Rita Dove. New York: HarperPerennial, 1990.

―――. *Moses, Man of the Mountain.* 1939. Foreword by Deborah E. McDowell. New York: HarperPerennial, 1991.

―――. "Songs of Worship to Voodoo Gods." *Zora Neale Hurston: Folklore, Memoirs, and Other Writings.* New York: Library of America, 1995. 533-55.

―――. *Their Eyes Were Watching God.* Foreword by Mary Helen Washington. Afterword by Henry Louis Gates, Jr. New York: J. P. Lippincott, 1937; Perennial Classics, HarperCollins, 1990.

―――. *Tell My Horse.* In *Zora Neale Hurston: Folklore, Memoirs, and Other Writings.* New York: Library of America, 1995. 376-97.

————. "Testimony." *Every Tongue Got to Confess: Negro Folk-Tales from the Gulf States.* Edited by Carla Kaplan. New York: HarperCollins, 2001. 22-23.

————. *Zora Neale Hurston: Folklore, Memoirs, and Other Writings.* New York: Library of America, 1995.

Johnson, Barbara. "Metaphor, Metonymy and Voice in *Their Eyes Were Watching God*." *Black Literature and Literary Theory.* Edited by Henry Louis Gates, Jr. New York: Methuen, 1984.

Jordan, Jennifer. "Feminist Fantasies: Zora Neale Hurston's *Their Eyes Were Watching God*." *Tulsa Studies in Women's Literature* 7 (Spring 1988).

Kirkham, E. Bruce. The Building of *Uncle Tom's Cabin.* Knoxville: University of Tennessee Press, 1977.

Lamothe, Daphne. "Vodou Imagery, African American Tradition, and Cultured Transformation in Zora Neale Hurston's *Their Eyes Were Watching God*." *Callaloo* 22, no. 1 (1999): 157-75.

Lillios, Anna. "'The Monstropolous Beast': The Hurricane in Zora Neale Hurston's *Their Eyes Were Watching God*." *The Southern Quarterly* 36, no. 3 (Spring 1998): 89-93.

Lizardi, José Joaquin Fernández de Lizardi. *The Mangy Parrot: The Life and Times of Periquillo Sarniento.* Written by Himself for His Children. Translated by David Frye. Indianapolis: Hackett, 2004.

————. *El Periquillo Sarniento.* New York: Appleton-Century-Crofts, 1952.

Lowe, John. *Jump at the Sun: Zora Neale Hurston's Cosmic Comedy.* Urbana: University of Illinois Press, 1994.

Magny, Claude-Edmonde. *The Age of the American Novel: The Film Aesthetic of Fiction between the Two Wars.* [*L'Age du roman américain.* Paris, 1948]. Translated by Eleanor Hochman. New York: Ungar, 1972.

Mallios, Peter Lancelot. "Tragic Constitution: United States Democracy and Its Discontents." *PMLA* 129 (Oct. 2014): 708-726.

Mariano, Trinyan. "The Law of Torts and the Logic of Lynching in Charles Chestnutt's *The Marrow of Tradition*." *PMLA* 128 (May 2013): 559-74.

Meisenhelder, Susan Edwards. *Hitting a Straight Lick with a Crooked Stick: Race and Gender in the Work of Zora Neale Hurston.* Tuscaloosa and London: University of Alabama Press, 1999.

Menchaca, Martha. *Recovering History, Constructing Race: The Indian, Black, and White Roots of Mexican Americans.* Austin: University of Texas Press, 2001.

Metraux, Alfred. *Voodoo in Haiti.* Trans. Hugo Charteris. New York: Schocken, 1972.

Mikell, Gwendolyn. "Feminism and Black Culture in the Ethnography of Zora Neale Hurston." *African-American Pioneers in Anthropology.* Edited by Ira E. Harrison and Faye V. Harrison. Urbana and Chicago: University of Illinois Press, 1999. 51-69.

Millward, David. "Obama warns of American legacy of racism." *The Telegraph.* 5 May 2015. 6:09 AM. British Standard Time. 5 May 2015. Web. 6 May 2015.

Moers, Ellen. *Harriet Beecher Stowe and American Literature.* Hartford: Stowe-Day Foundation, 1978.

Nicol, Abioseh. "The Meaning of Africa." *Africa Is Thunder and Wonder: Contemporary Voices from African Literature.* Ed. Barbara Nolen. New York: Scribner, 1972. 9-10. Rpt. of "The Continent That Lies Within Us." By Davidson [Aioseh] Nicol. *An Anthology of West African Verse.* Compiled by Olumbe Bassir. Ibadan, Nigeria: Ibadan University Press, 1957. 63-66.

Okada, Sumie. *Japanese Writers and the West.* New York: Palgrave Macmillan, 2003.

Owusu, Heike. *Voodoo Rituals: A User's Guide.* New York: Sterling, 2002.

Pastras, Phil. *Dead Man Blues: Jelly Roll Morton Way Out West.* Berkeley and Los Angeles: University of California Press, 2001.

Pavlic, Edward M. "Papa Legba, Ouvrier Barriere Por Moi' Esu in Their Eyes and Zora Neale Hurston's Diasporic Modernism." *African American Review* 38, no. 1 (2004): 61-85.

Pinckney, Josephine. "A Pungent, Poetic Novel about Negroes [Review of *Jonah's Gourd Vine*]." *New York Herald Tribune Books* (6 May 1934): 7. Rpt. *Critical Essays on Zora Neale Hurston.* Edited by Gloria L. Cronin. New York: G. K. Hall, 1998. 33-34.

Plant, Deborah G. *Zora Neale Hurston: A Biography of the Spirit.* Westport: Praeger, 2007.

Raffel, Burton, ed. Introduction. *The Tragedy of Hamlet: Prince of Denmark.* By William Shakespeare. New Haven: Yale University Press, 2003. xiii-xxix.

"Remembering 'Top Gun' Director Tony Scott." All Things Considered. National Public Radio. 20 Aug. 2012. Literature Resource Center. Web. 5 May 2015.

Rulfo, Juan. *The Burning Plain and Other Stories.* 1967. Translated by George D. Schade. Austin: University of Texas Press, 2008.

———. *Los Cuadernos de Juan Rulfo.* Edited by Clara Aparicio de Rulfo and Yvette Jiménez de Báez. Mexico City: Era, 1995.

———. *Pedro Páramo.* 1994. Translated by Margaret Sayers Peden. Evanston: Northwestern University Press, 1994.

Shakespeare, William. *The Tragedy of Hamlet: Prince of Denmark.* The Annotated Shakespeare. Edited by Burton Raffel. New Haven: Yale University Press, 2003.

The Skeleton Key. Dir. Iain Softley. Perf. Kate Hudson, Gena Rowlands, John Hurt, Joy Bryant, Maxine Barnett, and Bill H. McKenzie. Universal Pictures, 2005. DVD. 104 minutes. Color. Languages: English, Español, Français. Dolby digital 5.1.

Smith, Alexander McCall. *The No. 1 Ladies' Detective Agency.* Edinburgh, Scotland: Polygon, 1998; New York and Toronto: Random, Anchor, 2002.

Southerland, Ellease. "The Influence of Voodoo on the Fiction of Zora Neale Hurston." In *Sturdy Black Bridges: Visions of Black Women in Literature.* Edited by Roseann P. Bell, Bettye J. Parker, and Beverly Guy-Sheftall. Garden City, NY: Anchor, 1979. 172-83.

Starkie, Walter. Introduction. *Don Quixote of La Mancha.* By Miguel de Cervantes Saavedra. Translated by Walter Starkie. New York: Signet, 1964.

Stavans, Ilan. Introduction. *The Plain in Flames.* Translated by Ilan Stavans with Harold Augenbraum. Austin: University of Texas Press, 2012. Ix-xvi.

Stowe, Harriet Beecher. *Uncle Tom's Cabin; or Life among the Lowly.* Cambridge: Harvard University Press, 2009.

Sturluson, Snorri. *The Prose Edda: Norse Mythology.* Translated by Jesse L. Byock. London and New York: Penguin, 2005.

Their Eyes Were Watching God. Directed by Darnell Martin. Story by Zora Neale Hurston. Produced by Oprah Winfrey, Quincy Jones, Matthew Carlisle. Presented by Oprah Winfrey for Harpo Productions. Starring Halle Berry (Janie Mae Crawford), Ruben Santiago-Hudson (Joe Starks), Michael Ealy (Tea Cake), Ruby Dee (Nanny Crawford), and Mel Winkler (Logan Killicks), with Clarence Howard (Amos Hicks), Nicole "Nicki" Micheaux (Phoebe Watson), Gabriel Casseus (Sam Watson), Jensen Atwood (Johnny Taylor), Wayne Duvall (Dr. Simmons), and Artel Kayàru (Motor Boat). Screenplay Adaptation (Teleplay) Written by Suzan-Lori Parks, Misan Sagay, and Bobby Smith, Jr. Edited (Motion Picture for Commercial Television) by Peter C. Frank. Music by Terence Blanchard. Distributed by American Broadcasting Company (Disney—ABC Television Group), Harpo Films, and Touchstone Television Productions, 9:00 P.M., March 16, 2005.

Thomas, Hugh. *Conquest: Montezuma, Cortés, and the Fall of Old Mexico.* 1993. New York: Simon and Schuster, 2005.

Tucker, Glenn. *High Tide at Gettysburg: The Campaign in Pennsylvania.* Old Saybrook, CT: Konecky and Konecky, n.d.

Twain, Mark. *The Adventures of Huckleberry Finn.* London, 1884. New York and London: Sterling, 2006.

Vogeley, Nancy J. *Lizardi and the Birth of the Novel in Spanish America.* Gainesville: University Press of Florida, 2001.

Vogt, Wolfgang. *Juan Rulfo y el Sur de Jalisco: Aspectos de su vida y obra.* Guadalajara: El Colegio de Jalisco, 1992; Agata, 1994.

Walker, Alice. "Looking for Zora." 1975. *The Best American Essays of the Century.* Edited by Joyce Carol Oates and Robert Atwan. Boston: Houghton Mifflin, 2000. 395-411.

———. "Zora Neale Hurston: A Cautionary Tale and A Partisan View." Foreword. *Zora Neale Hurston: A Literary Biography.* By Robert Hemenway. Urbana: University of Illinois Press, 1977. Rpt. *In Search of Our Mothers' Gardens: Womanist Prose.* San Diego, New York, London: Harcourt Brace, 1983. 83-92.

Watanabe, Nancy Ann. *Beloved Image: The Drama of W. B. Yeats 1865-1939*. Lanham, New York, London: University Press of America, 1995.

———. "Hrotsvit (Roswitha; Hrotswitha) of Gandersheim." *New Catholic Encyclopedia: Supplement 2011: Art, Music, and Literature*. 2 vols. Edited by Robert L. Fastiggi. Washington: Catholic University of America Press; Detroit: Gale, 2011. 2: 341-43.

———. "Native Vision: Yeats's Tower (*The Dreaming of the Bones*) and Walcott's Harbor (*Dream on Monkey Mountain*)." *W. B. Yeats and Postcolonialism*. Edited by Deborah Fleming. West Cornwall: Locust Hill Press, 2001. 143-65.

Wheatley, Phillis. "On Being Brought from Africa to America." *The Norton Anthology of African American Literature*. Edited by Henry Louis Gates, Jr. and Nellie Y. McKay. New York: W. W. Norton & Company, 1996. 171.

———. *Poems on Various Subjects, Religious and Moral*. London 1773. Rpt. Philadelphia: Joseph Crukshank, 1789. Microform.

———. *Poems on Various Subjects, Religious and Moral*. *The Norton Anthology of African American Literature*. Edited by Henry Louis Gates, Jr. and Nellie Y. McKay. New York: W. W. Norton & Company, 1996. 167-78.

Zavala, Hernán Lara. "A golpe de martilla" / "Hammering Away." Translated by Pamela Carmell. *Best of Contemporary Mexican Fiction*. Edited by Álvaro Uribe with Olivia Sears. Champaign, IL: Dalkey Archive, 2009. 434-49.

"Zora Neale Hurston." *The Norton Anthology of African American Literature*. Edited by Henry Louis Gates, Jr., and Nellie Y. McKay. New York and London: W. W. Norton, 1997. 996-1065.